MW01166252

MAKING SHIFTS IN WAVES OF CHANGE

(A Coach Approach To Soulful-Leadership)

Edward H. Hammett

James R. Pierce

Email us at MakingShiftsinWaves@gmail.com
FB page: Making Shifts in Waves of Change

Author's Tranquility Press
ATLANTA, GEORGIA

Edward H. Hammett; James R. Pierce/Author's Tranquility Press
3800 Camp Creek Pkwy. SW Bldg. 1400-116 #1255
Atlanta, GA 30331
www.authorstranquilitypress.com

Publisher's Note: This is not a work of fiction.

Ordering Information:
Quantity sales. Special discounts are available on quantity purchases by corporations, associations, and others. For details, contact the "Special Sales Department" at the address above.

MAKING SHIFTS IN WAVES OF CHANGE/Edward Hammett; James R. Pierce
Hardback: 978-1-961908-24-6
Paperback: 978-1-961908-25-3
eBook: 978-1-961908-26-0

Scripture quotations marked KJV are from the Holy Bible, King James Version (Authorized Version). First published in 1611. Quoted from the KJV Classic Reference Bible, Copyright © 1983 by The Zondervan Corporation

Making Shifts In Waves of Change speaks to businesses, health care, profit and non-profit leaders

"Church leaders who take seriously the call to be 'salt and light', to equip their congregations to transform their community in the Spirit of Christ, need new approaches to leadership in our rapidly changing times. These authors command a profound grasp of both the 'way' and the 'how'. This book makes an extremely valuable contribution to this critical and timely topic."

—Larry Hovis, Executive Coordinator, Cooperative Baptist Fellowship of North Carolina

"Hammett and Pierce offer great insights for anyone involved in helping people, businesses, churches, and organizations navigate change. As a missional strategy leader, I found the 'coach approach' to change helpful to me as an organizational leader. The practical insights, the excellent coaching tools, and easy-to-read style make this book a must for any agent of change."

—Lonnie Reynolds, Author of Bridges: From Our World to Theirs

"The coach approach is truly a forward-moving process that can help leaders develop the centered focus they need to create change and prevent sabotage. Randy and Eddie have given us an important and challenging work that can provide individuals and systems with the survival tools needed during these fast-moving times. This is a valuable resource!"

—Patricia Doherty, Nurse Manager, Arbour Health Systems

"Making Shifts frames concepts of powerful and transformational coaching experiences I can testify work! Eddie's approach to coaching is unique and effective. I have been able to break free from self-imposed limitations and develop a stronger sense of self-belief and confidence. With Eddie's guidance, I've learned valuable strategies for maintaining focus, setting achievable goals, and overcoming obstacles. He has a remarkable ability to guide me towards solutions and insights that I might not have discovered on my own. His deep understanding and empathy create a safe and nurturing space where I feel comfortable exploring my thoughts and feelings.

Thanks to Eddie's coaching, I've not only achieved professional success but also experienced significant personal growth. I now approach challenges with a more positive mindset and am more resilient in the face of setbacks."

—**Linton Johnson,**
Founder and CEO, Ovis. News

"When congregations and other Christian organizations are ready for transformation, they need a coach approach to soulful-leadership for the transitions and changes they must experience. Eddie and Randy present a timely and excellent model and very practical tools for making significant shifts in the midst or waves of rapid changes. Read, practice, and feel the rust of soulful-leadership!"

—**George Bullard,**
Author, Coach, Consultant

"The leadership principles outlined here are applicable to a variety of organization, but I would hope church leaders will pay careful attention and learn well this coaching model. This book is a most helpful resource to equip leaders with skills for asking questions and pointing the way forward in this twenty-first-century world. This 'tool kit' will provide what is necessary for the task ahead, and the soulful-leader will discover fresh insights for bold leadership."

—**Bishop Larry M. Goodpaster,** The United Methodist
Church,
Western North Carolina Conference

"Our world is undergoing massive waves of change and this book by Edward Hammett and James Pierce is the perfect guide towards helping individuals, organizations, and congregations navigate these changes. The way forward and through is not by command and control or decree from on high. Rather, the way forward will be led by those who know how to coach organizations and individuals through a process of awareness and discovery so that they are empowered to discover their own creativity and action. Sharing their expertise in coaching and organizational understanding, the authors come alongside the reader and offer a guide that will empower and encourage the individual and organization to jump into the deep and face these waves of change - all with hope and without losing one's soul in the process. The genius of this book is that it is both conceptual and practical at the same time, and accessible to anyone who chooses to engage it. Well done!"

— **Scott Wagoner**
Quaker Pastor and Associate Certified Coach **(ACC)** with
International Coaching Federation **(ICF)**, Retreat Leader and
Congregational Coach.

"I love the HARMONY Model. It is an iron clad framework for any organization navigating change with the desire to foster a collaborative and culture-empowering environment. It shows leaders how to leverage the tide of change to lift all employees and partners to the next level of organizational success together in the most harmonious and inclusive fashion."

—**Dawn Hancock**, mipoh *(mipoh.com)*
Founder, Presenter and Thought Leader

"What's needed today are leaders who move us ahead without wrecking things. As Eddie and Randy demonstrate, leaders who take a coach approach are ably equipped to do this. For leaders and Organization who want to realize results and reduce the risks inherent to progress, this is a must-read."

—**Chad Hall, MCC, Founder and Executive Leader**
for Coach Approach Ministries and Author of *Faith Coaching*

CONTENTS

FOREWORD

When I was first married, my father-in-law gave me a large Craftsman tool kit, with every imaginable device that this master mechanic dad could imagine. This was the very image that came to mind as I read through the gift from these two masterful coaches!

Having personally journeyed with one of the authors as a participant and benefactor in the craft for some 25 years, I found the book to be a quite practical read and it certainly fulfills all the title's claim.

The interesting part of the book is that the reader not only benefits from the content but the internal coaching dialogue that the book generates within the reader.

As to the appropriate audience, I found it beneficial for application to families, places of worship, nonprofits, businesses, individuals and organizations of all sizes.

In so many ways the reader gains both knowledge and application tools while becoming the PBC (person being coached) by the end of this well-crafted gift to the coaching profession. Without realizing until late in the read, one is personally benefited for having read the book and by way of that experience acquires a heightened capacity regardless of whether seasoned sage or aspiring coach.

As I read the early manuscript, I could hear the gentle, patience, soulful, clarity and focus which I have grown accustomed to in my conversations with the author, now approaching 25 years of skillful mentoring!

John Bost
Master Counsel & Associates, Inc.
www.johnthecatalyst.com

Section I

Critical Times Calls for
Soulful-Leadership

ACKNOWLEDGMENTS

A lifetime of learnings and experiences frame the concepts of *Making Shifts In Waves of Change: A Coach Approach to Soulful-Leadership.* The powerful and life-changing realities of transforming soulful-leadership have touched us and challenged us to a transformed life and career that allows us to share these learnings with you.

For all those who have helped us learn, we are indebted. We have worked with organizations in the profit and non-profit worlds. Churches, businesses, and non-profit organizations have been our laboratories for over three decades. We have coached teams, organizations of many sizes and with a variety of mission statements.

We are also indebted to our families and many colleagues and friends who have been sounding boards, critics, and nurturers of this project. Encouragement and support are often needed while writing a book, and we are blessed.

Those who gave their endorsement brought their critical eye and years of experience to the reading and evaluating of this manuscript. These professional colleagues represent expertise in a variety of arenas of life. For their willingness to give their endorsements, we are deeply grateful.

Finally, without the professional coach training and coaching colleagues, this manuscript content would have never materialized. Linda Miller (MCC), Jane Creswell (MCC), Suzanne Goebel (PCC), Chad Hall (MCC), Bill Copper

(PCC), Marcia Reynolds, David Drake and Worldwide Business Executive Coaching Summit (WBECS), many of these powerful discoveries would have never been encountered and embraced in our lives. Thanks to these soulful leaders who shared their lives and learnings with us over the last decade.

***

My (*Randy*) journey has taken me down many different roads. I would like to thank Don Rainey, Lisa Phillips for the fantastic early days of my career at DaVinci Systems. Patricia Doherty at Arbour Hospital and Patty Evans at Aspen Education Group, gave me the opportunity to serve in our clinical professional world.

Sharon Kormendi, Josie Marshburn, Beverly Lock and Moriah Karalexis, our time and growth together at Oracle challenged us all to be and do better. It was "lighting in a bottle". Thank you for allowing me to be a part of your soulful-leadership.

And to you, Eddie Hammett, I would not be here today without you. Thank you for your coaching and love for over 25+ years now. You never gave up on me! Lastly, to David, thank you for your unconditional love and being my best friend.

We also want to thank Jade Freeman, his colleagues at Authors Tranquility Press for working diligently and professionally to get this book in print quickly.

PREFACE

The Impact of the Waves of Change

While finalizing this manuscript, Titanic Oceangate Submarine imploded seeking to visit the Titanic in the depths of the sea. All five passengers died because they ignored the safety warnings that had been voiced for years in efforts to get passengers inside the vehicle for exploring. They denied that an implosion of their dream could become a reality. Many organizations face similar situations in today's world filled with rapid change. Such changed families, schedules, medical communities, and even the court systems. The pandemic has subsided, but the grief, loss, and mental and physical stress effects continue to be hurdles to cross and adjustments to be made. The coach approach allows leaders to Make Shifts in Waves of Change!

Change shows up in the last decades in visible and challenging ways. We are still learning to face change with courage, creativity, curiosity and determination. Recall President Barack Obama declared, "Change has come to America" to describe the political reality brought about by his election in November 2008.[1] But his words could be applied to nearly every area of life over the past decade.

---

[1] Barack Obama, "Remarks of President-Elect Barack Obama: Election Night" (speech, Chicago, Ill., Nov. 4, 2008), Text can be found at http://www.barackobama.com/2008/11/04/remarks_of_presidentelect_bara.php, Video can be found at http://www.youtube.com/watch?v=HfHbw3n0EIM&.

Baby boomers are aging. A younger generation of leaders thinks about and values different perspectives and issues than their predecessors. It seems that "going green" is at the top of the agenda for many organizations, households and businesses. Women are stepping into an increasing number of leadership roles in government, education, medicine and economics. Yes, the world is shifting.

In these and other ways, most profit and non-profit organizations, businesses, families, employees, churches, and denominations are experiencing exponential waves of change, creating shifts of focus, energies, resources and/or personnel. Technology continues to impact us all, from iPhones to artificial intelligence (AI) to computers of every size, shape, and function. Now we are even seeing hints of holographic technology. An increasing number of meetings are being held online. Such new waves create new challenges that move us to a greater need for efficiency, effectiveness and timeliness. On-demand learning and steep learning curves face every person, institution, business and organization.

Making Shifts In Waves of Change: A Coach Approach to Soulful-Leadership recognizes that these historic shifts will create waves that challenge and waves that create new opportunity. The waves are certain to call for shifts in the way we view things and accomplish objectives. Regardless of whether you are churched or unchurched; Anglo, African American, Hispanic, Italian, Indian, Korean, Asian or Latino; rich or poor; Republican, independent or Democrat — change is here, and we will all continue to be touched in one way or another over the next decades. The reality is that this is what we face as families, businesses, churches, non-profit organizations, government agencies, schools and communities.

We believe a soulful-leader is a person who desires and is equipped for transforming influence and has transformational impact. As a result, people, organizations, families and businesses successfully encounter waves and experience shifts. We further believe that transformational impact can only occur after tough decisions are made and attitudes and behaviors are changed. This leads to the transitional steps in individuals and organizations that yield revolutionary transformation. You might even say that Revolutionary Transformation = Change + Transition.

The Influence of the Shifts Happening

The realities of today's and tomorrow's culture include a graying and a secularization of America. Our demographics are shifting toward people of color from white Anglo Saxon Protestants. The poor and the wealthy segments of the population are increasing and the middle class seems to be disappearing. In 2008, the financial industry experienced a meltdown, the price of oil skyrocketed, and families and businesses experienced overwhelming challenges. We are seeing this again today with Silicon Valley Bank and Signature Bank. Health concerns, education challenges, relational and family issues abound in every community. Fewer and fewer are honoring the sacred vows of marriage. Family life is becoming more and more based on relationships rather than blood, legal or religious commitments. Interracial and multicultural relationships are growing, creating challenges and difficulties for some. The world also faces what some see as "global warming," but others deny. Diversity of opinions and alignments are prevalent, so every family, organization, institution, church and government faces many waves of change and challenge that will call for shifts that some will embrace easily and others will resist. Obama's election, along with many other new realities, calls forth the best in us if we are to move forward rather than get trapped in blame games or hostilities. Making Shifts IN Waves of Change provides tools, coaching models, and insights for leaders and organizations that will strengthen our unity around issues of hope, healing, health, and desires to be better, not bitter.

The elections and the other new cultural and educational realities represent a seismic shift in our country. The political and cultural polarization and debate about 'culture wars' are stretching and stressing our communities and workplaces. We now have an opportunity to move forward, but new skills are required. Challenging external realities are calling forth internal shifts that can propel leaders and organizations to flourish in this time of change and challenge rather than build fortresses and barriers that threaten the very fabric of who we are and who we desire to become.

The Internet and artificial intelligence (AI), for the first time, proved to be a significant force in raising funds for political purposes, engaging the younger generation in a political movement. Worldwide formal and informal dialogues, blogs and online forums shaped and reshaped our

political and cultural landscape in ways that will be felt for at
least the next decade.

The stress and challenge of change are everywhere. It
gives us a powerful gift and an opportunity to build bridges
instead of barriers with other ethnic groups, economic
realities, relational challenges, and faith perspectives.
History is clear that change creates challenges, but it also
generates opportunity and momentum when people decide to
move forward. This is the hope, message, and toolkit Making
Shifts IN Waves of Change offers to you.

The Impact and Influence
of Soulful-Leaders

Consider your organization, your leadership style, your
value system, and your dreams and desires. How can you be
effective, successful, and all that God intends you to be in this
day of change and challenge? That is the focus of Making
Shifts in Waves of Change: A Coach Approach to Soulful-
Leadership. Our book offers a coach approach to introducing
and managing change and provides tools for making a soulful-
leader and soulful organization. The models, tools, skills and
encouragement we offer will help you face change with
courage, hope, health and clarity. This will allow you to build
ownership of the next steps for your family, organization,
faith group, or yourself as a leader. The challenge we now face
is how to become soulful-leaders of soulful organizations that
generate transforming influence and impact because of who
we are and what our destiny holds.

Edward (Eddie) H. Hammett, James R.(Randy)Pierce
(Email us at MakingShiftsinWaves@gmail.com)

(FB page: Making Shifts in Waves of Change)

June 23, 2023

INTRODUCTION

Today's changing world makes many uncomfortable. Consider these examples.

- Businesses compete for new ideas, productive products, and an efficient workforce. They're forced to do more with less in a shaky economy.

- Families experience an increasing number of pressures. Diverse family relationships, economic challenges, fast-paced lives, and stressors are around most corners, making it difficult for families to maintain balance.

- Schools seek more efficient, cost-effective ways of educating the existing and future generations. Learning styles are more varied than ever.

- Churches experience generational distinctive and a host of personal preferences of worship styles, learning styles, and values about the role of spiritual formation in life. Denominational loyalty rapidly declines while new networks of mission activity and support grow.

- Other non-profit and mission-driven companies struggle with volunteer enlistment, creative fundraising, and sponsorships and doing more with less.

  Amidst all this, change and transition are consistent threads.

- Adjusting to change is inevitable to move forward, but it requires courage.

- New disciplines, higher awareness, spiritual discernment, and new learning styles are needed to activate that courage. Leaders struggle with how to deal with overwhelming newness driven by technological advances (ChatGPT and Bard), economic shifts, and generational differences. Most want to keep their current clients or members happy, fearing a loss of support from over-challenging them.

- But churches and other organizations realize they must attract and learn to serve the younger generations effectively if they are to maintain their customer or membership base in the future.

- Many schools, universities, social and business gatherings moved to 'hybrid models' of gathering. Some are on media platforms, while some are 'in the office or school'. Such shift families, budgets, workstyles, and educational models! We continue to learn, grow and face challenges while discovering new opportunities

The issue then becomes for all, how do you make needed shifts without making too many waves? How do you move an organization, family, business, church, or denomination from just maintenance values to those of forward movement and mission? This question is partially fueling the growing movement of spirituality in the workplace. Companies and leaders of companies are seeking ways to recapture integrity and balance in life and work.

In Megatrends 2010, the author has a list of 7 megatrends – two of which are specific to spirituality in the business world 1) The Power of Spirituality; 4) Spirituality in Business. The other five trends relate to values, influence, and moral authority.[2]

The coach approach offers committed soulful-leaders and organizations a skill set and perspective that is based on discernment, hope, future progress, and actions that are decided and made through consensus and ownership of a next step. While it is unrealistic to think there will be no waves amidst change, it is also certain that not every person, group, or organization is best led by or open to the coach approach. It is certainly possible, with the coach approach, to build ownership of a new vision and make plans to enter that destiny with deep commitment. How possible is it? It is possible and probable.

The chart below can serve you and a good coach in doing some self assessment when it comes to probable shifts that are needed or in progress and how aware and open the group or individual is to making some of these shifts or some adaptation that is proper for their organization's progress. This New Communication Manifesto[3] frames "what's in" and "what's out" for persons in or working to communicate with

---

[2] Patricia Aburdene, *Megatrends 2010: The Rise of Conscious Capitalism*, (Charlottesville, Va.: Hampton Roads Publishing, 2005), xxi.
[3] Anders Gronstedt, "All Aboard! The Web 3D Train is Leaving the Station," T & D Magazine, (December 2008), 22-26, www.astd.org.

the digital generation (generally speaking those persons 40 and under).

The New Communication Manifesto
For the Digital Generation

What's Out	What's In
Legacy dogmas	New realities
Watching, reading and listening	Doing, simulating and engaging
Telling	Conversation and application
Sage-on-a-stage	Ubiquitous training
Command and control	Guide and nurture
Top-down	Peer-to-peer
Father knows best	Harnessing collective intelligence
Plan and execute	Release early and often, perpetual beta
Cautious and safe	Wacky and rebellious
Ask for permission	Ask for forgiveness
People going to training	Training going to people
Interruptive distractions	Teachable moments
Appointment-driven	On-demand
Captives in meetings	Communications in context
Graphic Design	Game Design
Efficiency and cost control	Effectiveness and Growth
Replicating communications with new media	Reinventing communications with new media
Compliance	Commitment

- What are your thoughts when you review this chart?

- What are three issues that you feel need to be considered seriously in order to increase your effectiveness as an individual or organization?
- What is needed to make these shifts?

We are keenly aware that this book promises much in the title. Our experience over the last decade of leadership in various organizations proves the power and practicality of the concepts we are introducing to you here. Throughout the book, you will find a sampling of powerful coaching. We will also be suggesting some reflective questions. These are keys to helping leaders and organizations make internal shifts so external and organizational shifts can happen without destructive waves of change but rather organized and predictable ripples of change.

Our suspicion is for many readers the previous list is more than overwhelming if not confusing and frustrating. Some will say, "I like things the way they are – why are these shifts needed?" Others will say, "The author of this chart 'gets it,' and we need to pay attention!" Such reactions simply illustrate the diversity of views and values in most organizations.

Our hope is that as you read this book, you might think of a pebble being thrown into a pond where ripples move from the inside to the outside. This image expresses how a soulful-leader that possesses good coaching and leadership skills can move from a dictated approach to change that usually makes waves to a collaborative approach that may have ripples but not overwhelming waves. That is the focus of this book and the drive that brought your authors to share, from our experience, practical and proven coaching steps of introducing and managing change without destroying your organization or your spirit.

(((•)))

CHAPTER ONE:

Making Shifts in Waves of Change— Is it Really Possible?

Change is like a storm

Change is like a storm that is crashing upon the shorelines of our time. We believe that while some ripples are inevitable, there are a variety of keys, strategies, and a leadership style for Making Shifts in Waves of Change.

In his book, The Church of the Perfect Storm[4], Leonard Sweet accurately calls the current environment "one of the greatest culture storms ever." In a review of the book on Amazon.com, George Bullard notes that organizations should prepare as ships get ready for a hurricane, heading out to sea to maneuver around the storm.

Many leaders today understand the forecast and recognize change as it makes landfall. Yet, knowledge itself is an inadequate instrument for navigating in the storm. Tools leaders once used to deal with incremental change no longer fit the massive shifts of today. Methods that worked ten, five, or

---

[4] Leonard Sweet, The Church of the Perfect Storm, (Nashville, TN: Abingdon Press, 2008), pg. 5

even two years ago are hopelessly out of date to deal with the exponential changes of our day. We believe that in this rapid paced culture of change, a leader trained to manage is not enough. Serious and challenging times call for a soulful-leader.

- Soulful-leaders trust their heart, intuition and curiosity as well as their knowledge – they integrate head and heart into leadership.

- Soulful-leaders push through their fears and understand the values of moving beyond their comfort zones.

- Soulful-leaders honor people and value their ideas during the process of change.

- Soulful-leaders work to lead by consensus when possible and believe that collaboration is more important than dictating mandates.

- Soulful-leaders trust methods but also trust their soul's voice as they use methods. The bottom line is important in leadership of any organization. Soulful-leaders value the divine alignments of their values and beliefs as well as how they live them out in times of change and challenge.

- Soulful-leaders value integrity and accountability.

- Soulful-leaders take action.

- Soulful-leaders take risks.

- Soulful-leaders are strategic.

Patricia Aburdene reminds us that "as individuals grow in consciousness and Spirit, so do the organizations they inhabit." She further clarifies, "The problem is organizations take longer to change than people do. Why is institutional change more difficult? Because it is so complex. Not only does it require time, vision, and leadership, but it involves a greater number of people, their commitment, and the development of a shared purpose. Institutional transformation relies on human evolution that grows slowly, then finally hits the mark."[5]

Even worse, old tools and outdated methods often cause more problems than they solve. It is becoming more and more challenging for leaders to lead their businesses or organizations; remain a student, themselves, for deeper learnings to sharpen their own skills; and stay abreast of all the constant changes. Cultural and global challenges abound, providing new horizons for most leaders and organizations. Walking into these waves without getting wiped out or consumed by rip tides is a skill. Learning to read the waves and time behaviors allows one to ride the waves, making the shifts that are needed. Leadership is critical, but the right leadership skills are even more critical regardless of the organization you are in or leading. It is increasingly important in the age of change for leaders not to just do things right, but to do the right things for the new emerging world.

---

[5] Aburdene, 2.

A New Perspective for New Challenges

A new approach is needed to help today's leaders make shifts in waves of change that do not destroy. One such approach can be found in the profession of coaching. The coach approach that has helped leaders focus their lives and find their purpose can help those same leaders manage their organizations through change.

Like a powerful hurricane levels anything else in its path, post-modernity, global economy, diversity in the workplace, changing family structures, and other issues are laying flat traditional thinking. And postmodernism and these other factors are growing rapidly. The most prevalent shifts are from propositional to experiential connections to truth; from individualistic to communal experiences; from theoretical to authentic values; and from naïve certainty to a deeper understanding of struggle. [6]When it comes to waves of change, sometimes there is a choice to make as to whether you accept the change and align yourself to it (i.e. it's cold or rainy, and you decide to wear a coat and take an umbrella). Other times, change presents itself in pressing waves that just do not subside, and a new reality has to be dealt with one way or the other (i.e. the circumstances surrounding all creating a 'new norm'; when North America shifted from agrarian culture to industrial to the printing press and now to the computers you can hold in your hand). People and organizations tend to feel the pinch of those waves of change that do not subside, and then the

---

[6] Don Everts and Doug Schaupp, I Once Was Lost: What Postmodern Skeptics Taught Us about Their Path to Jesus, (Downers Grove, IL: InterVarsity Press, 2008), xi.

intensity of the pinch and its consequences brings people and organizations to the point of making changes. Pain and constant discomfort often create an openness to change that otherwise would not have happened.

Sweet points out that people operating from a postmodern perspective have a loss of confidence in both pre-modern authority figures and modern reason. For post-moderns, he said it is less "Aha! Now I get it. I've figured it out" and more "Aha! Now I feel it. I've experienced exactly what you're talking about."[7] Added to the philosophical changes are major reality shifts. As of this writing, a sinking mortgage industry is creating ripples throughout the economy, family systems, educational systems, retail and the oil industry. The pinch is on.

Such change brings gale force uncertainty and surging uneasiness. The coach approach lets leaders put their organizational ship out to sea to maneuver in the storm, knowing that high winds and storm surges will damage any vessel moored in the port of predictability and the harbor of habit. Allowing this flexibility of movement and openness of pliability is needed for healthy, productive change.

Many leaders and organizations would like to avoid change, ignore the need, or deny the pressing realities and shifts around them. In fact, many have been in denial. That is why so many organizations and leaders have become irrelevant in the postmodern world. Now denial or avoidance is no longer an option. The waves are here, and the need for shifts is

---

[7] Leonard Sweet, The Church of the Perfect Storm, (Nashville, TN: Abingdon Press, 2008), 11.

paramount. Now we must face it – we're in the storm. We can let it destroy us, or we can learn to ride the waves of healthy change and transition.

Leaders using the coach approach help their organizations to not only weather the storm, but also to meet the challenge of making shifts without causing further destructive waves. Coaching allows the waves to subside to ripples that gradually create change.

Basic Coaching Concepts

This book is about using the coach approach to introduce and manage change in individuals, families, businesses, churches, non-profits, denominations, and communities. The skills we will discuss are appropriate and functional in any system or life that is coachable.

Determining coachability is critical. Using these skills in places that are not ready or healthy enough is likely to generate even more frustration. So, what makes a person, group, or system coachable?

- Open to change
- Ready to move forward
- Healthy enough to act responsibly and learn
- Driven by dreams and not by fears
- Commitment to the journey
- Understanding and open to help for others
- Willing to explore rather than avoid needed shifts

Perceptive leaders must determine the nature of change facing their organization and the coachability factor that is or is not present. Coaching provides practical means to make that call.

Effective leaders of 21st century groups must become familiar with the five coaching skills shown in the acrostic **LEARN**.

- **L**isten. Leaders should focus on what people in their organization are saying, paying careful attention to not only what they say but the way it is said. Leaders also need to be aware of what is not being said.

- **E**ncourage. Those at the head of a group must offer support that leads to action. Making mistakes is OK. It is part of the process.

- **A**sk questions. Leaders who want to know what's happening must ask powerful questions.

- **R**espond. Coaches are in the business of truth-telling. Leaders must offer feedback that moves the organization forward.

- **N**egotiate action. Every coaching conversation ends with the person being coached having clarity on what he or she is supposed to do and when it is supposed to be accomplished. Groups, families, businesses or churches that do not act will likely be swept away by the changing environment.[8]

These skills can be used in various models that can be adjusted to various situations. This basic model is used in most every coaching conversation or coaching relationship. Coaching conversations may be informal and brief. Coaching relationships are usually formal and involve a contract that is co-created with the person or group being coached.

While basic skills are presented here, we will build upon these in the pages to come as we apply these concepts to Making Shifts In Waves of Change. What then are the benefits of using the coach approach to introducing and managing change as opposed to a leader imposing or declaring change on an organization?

Benefits of Coaching

Coaching can help the church, families, or businesses reinvent themselves to weather the storms of change. Leaders who coach can help their organizations:
- Experience community, not cliques.
- Explore truth together and unlock passion.
- Move from indoctrination to inquiry.

---

[8] Acronym developed by Suzanne Gobel, PCC (www.theonpurposecompany.com), Jane Creswell, MCC (www.internal-impact.com) and Linda Miller, MCC (www.ca-ministries.com). Used by written permission.

- Build community through storytelling, personal expression and faith formation.
- Create a multi-sensory experience that becomes a sacred place and space for persons to explore deep questions, community and faith formation.
- Foster stewardship that nurtures life, personal mission and fulfillment of God's mission in the world
- Understand and embrace why change is needed.
- Encourage people to tell their stories and connect with the story of others.
- Draw out experiences of the heart rather than exercises of the head.
- Learning to weave relational, restorative and redemptive threads that become the fabric out of which authentic experiences emerge.

Advantages of Coaching

Coaching can have many advantages for organizations. Some can best be explained in our acrostic **COACHING.**

- Connections. Groups often function better when the members bond with each other. They do much greater things together than they could do alone. A leader serving as a coach helps the organization connect the dots of its problems, issues, and goals for movement forward.

- Options. A coaching relationship enables an organization to look at options more quickly. In many cases, organizations are stuck. Remaining in the same cycle produces no change. Frustration and hopelessness can build and take over.

- Action. The coach approach encourages groups to "bottom line" their learnings and moves them into action. In many cases, people know what they should or should not be doing but remain in a "no movement" zone. A coach adds a layer of accountability to the action.

- Community. In a group environment, the coach can serve as the connector and bridge builder to the entire team. Many who have been coached say they would have never moved as quickly or embraced change as effectively without being coached.

- Help. There is a surrender piece to coaching. Members of the group must get their egos out of the way, allowing themselves to be coached. Everyone needs help in areas of life. Clients and organizations must grant permission and show willingness to be stretched and step outside their comfort zones.

- Integration. A leader using the coach approach assists the group in the integration of their decisions. The leader-coach helps the group explore the pros and cons of changes and decisions. Life-changing transitions cause waves, and the shifts will need to be understood and embraced.

- Negotiation. The coaching environment enables members of the organization to realize where there is room to move and new areas to explore. Coaching will also enable them to list non-negotiables — places and things they are not willing to give up or change. A coach may or may not challenge some of the answers.

- Gifts. Coaching is about helping the group find its true potential, its calling and passions. Coaching is about helping the organization find healthy solutions and resources to move forward. Coaching helps plant seeds needed to build and grow with integrity and authenticity. Finding these gifts will enable everyone to feel truly alive and passionate for their contribution, efforts, and time. Jim Collins discusses "the Hedgehog concept" in his book, "*Good to Great.*" He states, "This concept is not a goal to be the best, a strategy to be the best, an intention to be the best, or a plan to be the best. It is an understanding of what you can be the best at. The distinction is absolutely crucial."[9]

Coaching is a powerful tool. We quickly acknowledge that trying to write about coaching brings its challenges. We are only able to jump-start coaching conversations or relationships with most of our writing because we do not have the other side of the conversation present. Coaches work off of the words and situation of the client. Coaches listen attentively, being fully present with the person or group being

---

[9] Jim Collins, *Good to Great*, (New York: Random House, 2001), 98.

coached. So know, much of what we introduce you to simply represent a way to jump-start coaching conversations, but nonetheless, the timely use of the concepts, tools and skills we share are powerful. Try it and see what happens. Here's something about my journey as I worked with these tools.

One Person Can Make a Difference!

So often, in the emotions that often surround change, tempers flare, personal conflicts emerge, and relationships often dissolve amidst differing personal agendas and efforts to "be right." The issue often can be bottom lined by the powerful question, "Do we want to be right, or do we want the relationship?" Notice as Eddie shares two powerful personal experiences how much power one person can have when seeking to make shifts without making waves.

One of the most powerful pieces of the *Reaching People Under 30 While Keeping People Over 60* book is my "grandmother story." After being invited to serve as a part-time staff person at my home church during my college years, I was assigned the responsibility of moving my grandmother's Sunday School class. This sounded simple enough to me since the fire marshall had declared that new rules required that our baby nursery be moved closer to an outside exit. My grandmother's class was near an exit, their room was much more spacious, and their membership was declining. Another factor here that assured me of the ease of this assignment was that most of the ladies in her class had diapered me in the nursery during my toddler years.

Suffice it to say that the idea, though practical and "required by the fire marshal," was not readily accepted by the Sunday School class. They had been in that room for several decades and had made it "their own." My grandmother was not happy either. So much so that she closed the door on our regular Sunday lunches at her house. She also declared that she and I would pray and dialogue to discover what could be done – now that I had "torn up her Sunday School class." Her wisdom guided our relationship for the next painful months. She eventually discovered and declared to me and to her peers, "I have come to understand that my (our) personal comfort is not as important as this church's mission." After revealing this new conviction to her fellow classmates, they picked up their chairs and moved to a small room and created space in their old room for a nursery that was growing. We never heard another complaint from them, and they became engaged in ministering to the newborns and their families.

Another personal illustration happened during the days when I (Eddie) was battling heart trouble and facing open heart surgery. My family's expectation was always that our pastor, or the pastors of family members who went to other churches, were to come and pray for those in our family who were about to go into surgery. I felt that this was no longer a wise expectation or need – our family could pray! So I called each pastor and asked them not to come to my bedside prior to surgery. After all, it was 5 a.m. in the morning. Our family and friends were present at my bedside that morning. Each began to ask, "Where's my pastor?" I revealed that I had asked them not to come. They seemed to understand my logic and wish. The next moments were some I would not trade for anything. I heard and observed our family make some very needed shifts in their pastoral expectations as we experienced some of the most powerful prayer times our family has every shared together! Now our family no longer has the pastoral expectation set – in fact, we celebrate where we can beat the pastor to bedside and pray ourselves.

Now granted I was not utilizing all of the powerful coaching skills in full in these scenarios. I was using the principles and questions we shared here. The impact was a transformational change of internal beliefs that impacted external behaviors and ultimately influenced and impacted others without creating tidal waves of emotions around emotionally volatile issues.

Most leaders want to make shifts without making waves. They don't want to hurt people or make people mad in the midst of change and transition, but it is often unavoidable. Leaders who constantly walk this tightrope can find in the coach approach principles, concepts, and insights to minimize personal and organizational trauma. The result will be a significant change that insures growth and progress.

Section II

The Impact of Soulful-Leadership

$(((\bullet)))$

CHAPTER TWO:

Soulful-Leadership Creates Transformation

Shifts happen. Some are planned. Others are unintentional. Some shifts are internal. They might be linked to self-image, openness to the Spirit, addictions, or belief systems. Others are external. They can occur after terrorist attacks, economic downturns, death, health problems, pandemics, or family challenges.

Before learning to handle shifts in waves of change, leaders must first acquire skills to make smooth the often turbulent journey. The coach approach offers such skills.

Attunement and Alignment?

The coach approach is a powerful leadership tool that honors the best in humans and believes that answers to life, career, economic, family, and relational challenges are found within as clarity is gained through reflection, exploration, and discernment. The coach approach is as concerned about attunement as it is alignment. Alignment is often about control and is usually forced. Attunement is more about seeing the value in the tough decisions needing to be made, building consensus, and adjusting out of desire to be "in tune" with others and the objectives being proposed. Attunement is not always a viable option for the decision-maker or employee when change comes. Coaching and soulful-leadership can explore the viability of attunement and make change and transitions more a work of transformation of heart and structure. Discovering and discerning these answers is the power of coaching, as it connects the mind, heart, and spirit. Jane Creswell explains in her book, Coaching for Excellence that "coaching is a brain-altering experience." The new insights you'll help people gain through your coaching create new synapses and neural pathways in their brains, and it's also a brain-altering experience for you, the coach. In order to coach others, you'll first have to clarify and adjust your assumptions about people.[10]

Shifts that the coach approach calls for and helps make a soulful-leader include the following:

- Ask, don't tell.
- Listen, don't talk.
- Rethink your value.
- Understand that your reactions reveal your worldview.[11]
- The person being coached (PBC) is responsible for his or her own learnings. Coaching is about helping people take responsibility for their lives and decisions. Coaches are guided by a differing set of skills and

---

[10] Jane Creswell, The Complete Idiot's Guide to Coaching for Excellence, (New York: Alpha Books/Penguin, 2008), 49.
[11] Creswell, 56-59.

values than most other consultants and facilitators. Coaching is distinctive in a variety of ways.

One such skill is discernment — the ability to forecast approaching storms, to understand the existing environment, and to read the oncoming waves. In short, the leader must recognize and understand the current reality. "Coaching is a positive approach that looks to the future. It is an accountability process that helps the person being coached set goals, find solutions, and make forward progress," Creswell says.[12]

This approach can also be applied to groups. Powerful questions can help the leader see the organization clearly to move the group forward toward its goals. Coaching is not about telling or directing. Consider these possible coaching questions.

- How would you describe our group?
- What's working?
- What would make the current situation better?
- What are we struggling with?
- What energizes us?
- What drains our energy?
- What would make things better?

---

[12] Creswell, 3.

A Metaphor for Coaching

Randy (James) relates how he was reminded of coaching's impact during a recent trip.

As I was arriving at the airport, I found myself once again in the long line going through security. I love watching people. It serves as a great coping skill while waiting for long lines to move. As I watched, more and more people became frustrated and agitated with the gridlock. People were taking laptops out of bags, slipping off shoes and belts, and checking each pocket twice. They placed their belongings in trays for the x-ray machines and then walked through the metal detectors. As the line began to move, I immediately observed the next person in line beginning to relax a bit as they took their appropriate action of the next steps to move them forward.

I simply grinned as I thought how similar it was to the impact of good coaching: taking action and moving forward. No one likes to feel stuck or, even worse, move backwards. Coaching is all about putting your thoughts, ideas and passions into action to get to the next step.

After making it through the security line, people want to quickly get to the next step of arriving at the gate, perhaps grabbing a paper, a quick beverage, a bite to eat, and a last bathroom stop before boarding the plane. Then in line to board the plane, the process starts again. People want to quickly board and get settled, being the first to claim an overhead spot for carry-on luggage, coats, and laptops. I observe again how people know where they want to go but wait for interference to get out of the way. In our lives, we sometimes need to move our own interference, but in this scenario, I would not recommend it. I don't think the person in front of you would be very happy if you executed a "block and tackle" move to simply get ahead in the boarding line. Once again, I observe more satisfaction as everyone participates in the next steps of movement to where they want to be.

On the plane, I noticed everyone's need and longing to stay connected. Everyone sends their last text, email, or phone call before the announcement from the airline attendant to turn off all electronic devices. And, it almost never fails, someone on the plane needs two or three reminders to "wrap it up" and turn the device off with a stern look from the attendant. You know she is wondering why is there always one on every flight?

So, everyone is seated and thinks the plane is ready to take off. As we are sitting on the tarmac, the pilot announces that we are 10th in line. I immediately felt the energy shift on the plane as I heard sighs and soft moans. But, once the plane begins to move, there is again a feeling of progress, movement forward to where we all want to be. If you truly stop and allow yourself to observe this the next time you are traveling, you can honestly feel the shifts in the energy on the plane.

This is how coaching works. Coaching opens the process for self-discovery and a confidential relationship for connecting the dots for movement forward, unleashing one's potential to move interference out of the way and make things happen quickly.

The plane lands at our destination. As soon as the wheels hit the runway, everyone reaches to turn on their wireless devices. What emails, texts, and social posts has everyone missed? We all rush to be connected again to gather the data we need for our own next steps. Moving forward and staying connected, two main ingredients are necessary for effective coaching.

Leaders can use the necessary skills described in chapter one (LEARN skill set) to help their groups and individuals move forward and stay connected. Those skills come together in coaching models that can be found in coaching literature. However, there are basic concepts in most every coaching conversation or relationship. One model coaches use is best remembered by the acrostic **FAST**.[13]

- **Focus**. Coaches ask questions like, "What's on your mind today?" and "What do you want to accomplish during this conversation?" Leaders might ask questions like, "What do we need to accomplish?" and "What's the top issue facing us now?"

- **Action**. This determines what might be possible. Coaches ask questions such as "What have you thought about doing?" and "What might be your first step?" Leaders might ask, "What are our options?" and "What do we need to do?"

- **Summarize**. Connecting the dots of the conversation helps the person being coached to explore how the situation got to be where it is. Coaches ask questions like "How'd we get here?" Leaders can ask "What

---

[13] Framed and developed by Suzanne Goebel – www.theonpurposecompany.com.

caused the current situation?" Another coaching question may be, "Will you recap or bottom line your takeaways?"

- **Tracking**. This helps the person being coached to see the big picture. Coaches ask questions such as, "How does this play into your overall agenda?" Leaders might ask, "How does this fit into our mission?" Tracking is also used to bring in accountability. What is the client willing to do by the next coaching session?

Finding the Focus and Keeping It

A coach's most challenging function with an individual or group is to help the client find focus and keep it. In a busy world with so much stimuli and information, it is increasingly difficult for persons or organizations to focus enough to make decisions and move forward. In fact, focus is often the major issue that compels an organization to get a coach. Facilitators and consultants bring in more information. Coaches take the group's information and help focus it in ways that allow them to frame and work on their agenda for forward movement.

Focus is achieved through skillful listening and asking powerful questions along with tracking the information being shared. Some additional focusing questions might include:

- What would you like to talk about today?
- What would be most helpful to talk about now?
- Which piece of what you shared is most critical now?

- How would you prioritize the importance of those things you would like to discuss?
- Which of the top three would you like to resolve now?

Keeping focus is another challenge. The coach has to listen carefully for disconnects with the focused agenda when detours emerge. The coach has to determine if the information being shared is fruitful for the focused agenda, whether it's a personal agenda or a story that has little or no significance in moving forward. Then this observation needs to be checked with the group as a whole. The coach can make a decision, but it's best if this decision is embraced and made by a consensus of the group being coached.

The chart below is an adaptation of material often used in churches and non-profit organizations. The coach can use the chart when the group is struggling to determine core values or to explore if what is being said actually lines up with what is being done.

What is the focus of your organization?

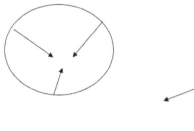 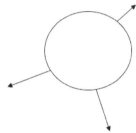

Attractional Organization **Missional Organization**

Attractional Organization	Missional Organization
Grow the organization	Impact the world/community
Time/tasks/Defined by (mission/objectives)	Restore/redeem broken people
Who is 'in/out' of the organization	Web of relationships inside and outside the organization
Fish to keep (rod and reel) membership for retention	Fish & release (net) membership for mission activation
Come structures that focus only on institutional preservations	Go structures that focus beyond the institution to the mission of the organization
Building buildings and more organizational structures	Building relationships and people inside and outside the organization
Bounded (fence-like characteristics)	Centered (like a well found in the midst of a desert)
Homogeneous	Diversity

Adapted by Edward Hammett from The Shaping of Things to Come: Innovation and Mission for the 21st Century Church by Michael Frost and Alan Hirsch, Hendrickson, 2003.

The above chart serves as a guide for the self-assessment of an individual, group, or organization. From a coach approach, the coach might simply provide the chart and ask the person or group being coached:

1. What category best describes your group/organization?
2. How would you evaluate your organization?
3. How does your daily activity attune with your previous answers?
4. How do your daily activities honor your mission statement?
5. What would help you to be more attuned as an organization now?
6. Who can help you make the needed shifts?
7. What are the shifts you believe need to be made to improve your effectiveness over the next six months?

The Case for Change in the Church and Organizations

These tools can be used in almost any organization. One group that serves as a prime example of their effectiveness is the church.

In his books *The Rise of the Creative Class, and The Flight of the Creative Class,* Richard Florida says most current institutions value things that turn away and discredit rather than nurture and cultivate those persons in what he calls the Creative Class[14], the innovators of our day.

Nowhere is that more evident today than the church and its failing organizations. They are barely weathering the culture storm of change as leaders often make more waves than they do shifts.

The church has refused to lift anchor as the storm hits, becoming a drag for many church people and effectively turning off the unchurched.

What's the problem? In a culture where spiritual thirst is at an all-time high and many are searching for meaning to life's challenges, why are many churched persons dropping out of church and why are many spiritual travelers not finding the church help in their spiritual journey?

Here are some of the things the church's own members say:

- "My church spends more time debating trivial issues (that we make big) than we spend discipling those who are spiritually hungry."

---

[14] Richard Florida, *The Flight of the Creative Class: The New Global Competition for Talent*, (New York city: HarperCollins, 2007), , and *The Rise of the Creative Class and How It's Transforming Work, Leisure and Everyday Life*, (New York: Perseus Books, 2004).

- "Why do many church people focus on preserving tradition rather than finding ways to penetrate the contemporary world with the Good News?"

- "I'm tired of fighting with church people about issues that those in the world we are supposed to be trying to reach find irrelevant."

- "My church refuses to rethink the way we do church and make it more relevant and convenient for my busy family. I have no choice but to drop out."

Other church members complain that the church has become miserable because things have changed. They say the church no longer pleases them or meets their needs.

Still, other church members say they became dissatisfied with the church when people, unlike them, started attending.

The unchurched are straightforward about their views. "Church people are more concerned about the church that pleases them than the church that is meaningful to me," one said. Also, in the business world, there's a pervasive cry for honesty, authenticity, integrity, and work that is meaningful. Authors like Ken Blanchard, Patrick Lencioni, Jane Creswell, John Trent, Linda Miller, Marcia Reynolds, Marshall Goldsmith, and John Maxwell address these and other principles in the business world. (*See appendecies for additional resources.*)

The Church in the Storm

Sweet notes in his book that Christians are "headed into one of the greatest culture storms ever"[15] but explains something of the value and history of storms for the church. According to Sweet, three category five storms are being faced by the church (and most organizations in our 2009 world) – all overlapping, mutually reinforcing, multiple storms to create collectively what sweet notes might be called the perfect storm.

1. Tsunami known as postmodernity.
2. The Big Hurricane, or more precisely an epidemic of related hurricanes, called post-Christendom.
3. Global warming.[16]

There is hope found in these storms of our time in history. Sweet recalls, "In both the book and the movie *The Perfect Storm*, there was one reason to go out into the storm and risk being lost at sea: to make the ultimate catch. Sweet argues, and we agree, that the perfect storm offers the church its greatest chance to become the "Ultimate Church" and make the ultimate catch for the gospel. (Similarly, companies have the opportunity to become the "Ultimate Company.") If churches can navigate this sea change, cross this "Red Sea," we will find a promised land of new beginnings and a new church on the other side. What is also certain is that the

---

[15] Sweet, 2
[16] Sweet, 4

future will be far better for the church than the past. What is also true is that many churches (*organizations/businesses*) will be left behind, smash on the shoals of status-quoism, or sink into oblivion."

Storms prune and purify. They tear down all that is not tied down and lasting. They enforce the rule of persevere or perish. It behooves us to make the most of our storms. For in the words of British Methodist Colin Morris in his book *Things Shaken – Things Unshaken: Reflections on Faith and Terror (London: Epworth Press, 2006),* "God wills a new creation which may be a gift from beyond history, the kingdom of heaven, but which is made up of elements from every era in history that have withstood the shaking, gone through the refiner's fire and had the dross burned off them."[17]

"When everyone and everything is spinning and whirling in the wind, Christians go out to meet the storm. Christians embrace the wind. And pass out kites."[18]

Whether a church, a non-profit group, a business, a family, or a community, storms are in our future – they can tip your boat over, or they can offer great, new challenging opportunities to move forward, develop new skills, new products, new ways of delivery and maybe even new clients, members or colleagues. For more on the subject, see *Note to*

---

[17] Colin Morris, Things Shaken – Things Unshaken: Reflections on Faith and Terror, (London: Epworth Press, 2006), 156, quoted in Sweet, 5.
[18] Sweet, 5.

Self by Andrea Buchanan (Simon Spotlight Entertainment, 2009).

What are you willing to learn from the storms or shifts life brings your way? How open are you to learning and facing steep learning curves with faith, courage, and hope?

(((•)))

CHAPTER THREE:

Soulful-Leaders Create Harmony Through Coaching

Change with integrity seems to be the cry of the day. Some want it; others resist it. Some seek to make it happen; still, others are tossed and turned because of it. We find it in politics, government, education, businesses, families, communities, economics, churches, and denominations. Since change seems to be everywhere these days, the challenge is to learn to create harmony without making too many waves or causing too much chaos.

Waves are inevitable in most climates and circumstances. Sometimes the waves bring energy that moves things that have been stationary for too long. Other times the waves bring a great force that destroys treasured possessions and dreams. At times we have the option of making waves that matter. Influencing the power of change is possible. People in times of hurricanes fill sandbags to redirect waves, withstand waves, and sometimes to prevent what seems like inevitable destruction. Similar possibilities exist for intentional leaders in organizations utilizing the coach approach to change. Obviously, in emergency circumstances, quick confrontation may be needed, not coaching. But if we could have the best of circumstances when change is called for, coaching offers powerful tools for *Making Shifts in Waves of Change.*

Rather than creating waves when shifts are presented how can leaders influence, open new doors, and rethink and refocus beliefs and priorities? A soulful-leader relies heavily upon the LEARN (Listen, Encourage, Ask, Respond, Negotiate) skills and basic coaching models such as FAST (Focus, Action, Summarize, Tracking) to coach persons forward who might be stuck and in a defensive posture.

Moving toward harmony and attunement or from maintenance to mission are often desired outcomes for families, organizations, churches or teams when difficulties known as "pinches" enter the picture.

For this reason, coaching is a profession and skill set whose time has come. People, businesses, and churches are searching for ways to save time, energy, and resources while at the same time moving forward and making adjustments in light of new knowledge and challenges. Coaches are confidential companions that move people and organizations from where they are to where they want to be. Coaching is about creating space so the transformation can happen. Whether you are coaching an individual or group you co-create transformation in an environment that is safe but challenging. This chapter speaks of the many shifts and skills — some internal and some external — needed by leaders and organizations to establish a coaching culture that will enable healthy and effective change rather than change that is disconcerting and painful.

Creating a Coaching Culture Facilitates Effective Change

No leader wants to create tension or dissension in his/her organization when change is needed. Dictatorial leaders just announce change and demand that others align themselves with it – or else. Laissez-faire leaders see the need and desire for change but are such people pleasers and dislike conflict so much that they often avoid change and frequently sabotage the potential of the organization. Soulful-leaders see the need for change, know that others need to have a voice in the change, and understand the need for others to buy into the change for the organization to flourish. Soulful-leaders engage others from the very beginning in evaluating the need for change, inviting them into the dialogue and giving them a voice in the plans as they are crafted. The soulful-leader empowers and encourages others to help implement the group's visions and decisions.

What needs to happen when using the coach approach for introducing and managing change? As stated earlier, the coach approach is not top-down commands for change but rather inviting others into the change process. Coaches hear what others think and consider what they feel needs to change. Coaches lead the group to assess needs, decide the sequence for change, build ownership, and evaluate the effectiveness of change. Creating a coaching culture in an organization might be summarized best in four powerful coaching questions:

- What's working
- What's not working?

- What will make it better?
- Who can champion the change needed now?

Facing the Challenge of the Coach Approach

Creating a coaching culture in an organization is worthy of another book in itself. Meanwhile, here are some pointers for working with an organization that seems coachable.

First, creating a coaching culture takes time. You begin with key people who are most coachable and interested in moving forward. Building *such* an atmosphere often requires a contract or covenant between those who show the most enthusiasm for change. They are enlisted to serve as internal coaches and become the first round of coach trainees who model for others the skill and impact of the coach approach.

Creating a coaching culture begins with the leadership, openness and coachability of the organization or group involved. The soulful leader is called to coach, not be a directive leader.

Soulful-leaders learn new skills and embrace their value in creating organizational advancements. A key challenge for the soulful-leader is being able to move from a "telling posture" to an "asking posture." That is, soulful-leaders no longer hand out orders. Instead they help people discover and take next steps.

Soulful-leaders are coaches who believe the best answers are within the collective voice of employees, clients, and members rather than from the edicts of just a board or staff directive.

Soulful-leaders are confident that the skills, insights, gifts, abilities and experiences of those they are leading are valuable in making things better and improving the quality of relationships, products or effort.

Soulful-leaders who are building a coaching culture also acknowledge that the passion and callings of those they lead is a critical part of moving the organization and system forward. They trust that the right persons are in the organization for taking the next steps. Steps that they can embrace, nurture and live into. *Good to Great*, Jim Collins' powerful book about organizational change, suggests that there are times when the "wrong people are on the bus" and therefore prohibit or sabotage change. If this is discovered he suggests getting the "wrong people off the bus and the right people on the bus." [19]While there may be times when this is unavoidable, we suggest that those wanting to create change through a coach approach take a different approach to dissenters.

---

[19] Adapted by Hammett & Pierce, Collins, pg. 55f

The Soulful-Leader's Response
to the Dissenters/Skeptics

Soulful-leaders understand what William Bridges calls a "neutral zone." Bridges says this "gap in the continuity of existence" comes about because "emptiness represents the absence of something."[20]

So when something is as important as relatedness and purpose and reality, we try to find ways of replacing these missing elements as quickly as possible," Bridges says. "The neutral zone is not an important part of the transitional process – it is only a temporary state of loss to be endured."[21]

We believe that this neutral zone creates time and space for rebirthing, personal reflection, meditation, and making shifts that matter. It's the time when you pay attention to "that new baby kicking" that allows you the space and opportunity to embrace the new and the risks of the new. It's the time that we have to self-manage ego and the demands of our fast-paced lives allowing us to pull forth new disciplines and new realities.

As a way of self-management, the soulful leader carefully considers the following questions. This opens the leader up to the reality that those who are skeptics might be good teachers who can strengthen the needed shifts being called for. Far too often, leaders consider those who oppose change as enemies

---

[20] William Bridges, Transitions: Making Sense of Life's Changes, (Reading, Mass.: Perseus Books, 1980), 112.
[21] Bridges, 112.

and threats rather than teachers and potential strategists who can help make the change more meaningful and relevant to the organization. As a soulful-leader consider these questions about those who seem opposed to change:

- What do they see that I do not see?
- What do they see that others do not see??
- What are the issues of most concern to them now? In the future?
- What can we learn from their concerns?
- What do they need to buy into the shifts?
- How can we create a win/win without sabotaging the mission?
- What's missing from the dialogue about change?
- How can those who are opposed to change or rocked by change move from pain to purpose to passion?
- What avenues can be created to relieve the pain and discomfort of change and open doors to renewed purpose and intense passion?

After personally reflecting on the skeptics and what they might be able to bring to the dialogue, those same questions can be reframed and asked directly of those who might be touched by change – directly or indirectly. The learnings from this internal and external dialogue is certain to bring greater clarity on most if not all the issues and build some ownership and practical solutions to the challenges and opportunities ahead.

Harmony emerges as opinions are shaped, voiced and heard. Effective soulful -leaders are called to be healthy and skilled coaches in times of stress and great diversity of opinion, demographics or value systems and traditions. Let's explore who a coach is, then delve deeper into what a coach does.

Coaches Step into Healthy Soulful-Leadership

Coaching demands great self-awareness and comfort with who you are as a leader. Coaches have a keen sensitivity and ability to read a group and move the group toward contextualized answers to their unique challenges.

Soulful-leadership must step up to the challenge of coaching and learning curves brought by change. Ruth Haley Barton discusses the challenges leaders often face. "Such moments come to all of us – moments when our leadership feels like something we 'put on' like a piece of clothing pulled out of the closet for a particular occasion rather than something that flows from a deep inner well fed by a pure source. Perhaps you are preparing a presentation, and you have the sinking realization that you are getting ready to exhort others in values and behaviors you are not living yourself. Maybe you are a leader and notice that, more and more frequently, you are manufacturing a display of emotion because it has been too long since you have experienced any real authenticity. Or perhaps someone needs care and you realize you just don't care. You rally your energy to go through the motions, but you know that your heart is devoid of real compassion."[22]

Soulful-leaders must walk into their discomfort and their fears to lead people and groups forward. Barton brings further clarification when she declares that "the soulful leader pays attention to such inner realities and the questions that they raise rather than ignoring them and continuing the charade or judging himself or herself harshly and thus cutting off the possibility of deeper awareness. Spiritual leadership emerges from our willingness to stay involved with our own soul – that place where God's Spirit is at work, stirring up our deepest questions and longings to draw us deeper into relationship. Staying involved with our soul is not narcissistic navel-gazing; rather, this kind of attentiveness helps us stay on the path of becoming our true self – a self that is capable of an ever-deepening yes to God's call on our life." Barton says "the settings in which many of us are trying to provide leadership are places where everyone is crashing through the woods together, harried and breathless, staying on the surface of the intellect and the ego while all things soulful flee deeper into the woods. Besides that, we know that the leader is often the one who gets shot or voted off the island. The savvy soul knows better than to run out into a clearing, thereby giving everyone a better shot!"[23]

Soulful-leadership that functions creatively and spiritually in the midst of paradox is not for the faint of heart.

---

[22] Ruth Haley Barton, Strengthening the Soul of Your Leadership: Seeking God in the Crucible of Ministry, (Downers Grove, IL: IVP Books, 2008), 23.
[23] Barton, 25-27.

It is much easier to give into one polarity or the other. Peter Senge notes in the *Fifth Discipline*, "Emotional tension can always be relieved by adjusting the one pole of the creative tension that is completely under our control at all times – the vision. The feelings that we dislike go away because the creative tension that was their source is reduced. Our goals are now much closer to our reality. Escaping emotional tension is easy – the only price we pay is abandoning what we truly want, our vision." A spiritual leader is not willing to merely escape the emotional tension; rather, he/she has the stamina and staying power to remain in that place of creative tension until a third way opens up that somehow honors both realities."[24]

A coach needs to be aware of these leadership characteristics in themselves and those they are coaching. A coach is called to self-manage personal agendas, opinions, and judgments when coaching. The person or group being coached dictates the agenda. The coach, however, listens and watches for patterns – what's working and what's not working, along with what is being avoided or ignored. The coach's job is to connect dots that move the person or group forward in their tasks.

In his book, *From Coaching: Evoking Excellence in Others*, James Flaherty says relationship is the first and most important principle in coaching. "Relationship is the background for all coaching efforts," he says. The relationship

---

[24] Peter M. Senge, The Fifth Discipline, (New York: Random House, 2006), 26.

must be one in which there is mutual respect, trust and mutual freedom of expression."[25]

Flaherty says the products of coaching include long-term excellent performance, self-correction, and self-generation. [26]

Distinctives of Leading Through Coaching

Let's unpack some of the distinctives of leading through coaching. How is coaching different from being a good leader? What would a soulful leader need to become an excellent coach? Some needed skills can be seen in how leaders FACE change, MAKE change, and EMBRACE change. Consider these options and the accompanying coaching questions.

Leaders must FACE change.

Coaching to **FACE** Change
- Fear
- Accept
- Community
- Evaluate/Explore

---

[25] James Flaherty, Coaching: Evoking Excellence in Others, (Boston: Butterworth Heinemann, 1999), 3.
[26] Flaherty, 3-4.

Fear - Fear is extremely powerful. Personal fear keeps you stuck. Fear can keep you in old patterns and habits that can sabotage the future, even pull you backward. It is human nature to remain in comfortable old familiar places, even if these places might be bad for us. Fear is the opposite of love. Looking at fear this way can help. It is quite more challenging than we think to truly love ourselves and allow good things to happen.

Iyanla Vanzant, a true inspirer and life coach, states, "People develop habits. They do certain things in certain ways, not because that is the only way they can be done. Rather they act in certain ways because human beings are habitual. Let's face it, we are easily trained, habitual creatures who become comfortable doing certain things in a particular way. If we want to be honest, we would have to admit that the way we do the things we do is more often than not an attempt to avoid pain, discomfort, and unfamiliarity, not necessarily in pursuit of doing things the best way or the right way — if there is such a thing. Taking this into consideration, we can honestly say that as human beings, we don't always do the right thing. We cut corners. We tell little fibs. We do what we think we must do to save ourselves. We react to many life situations in fear, with a fear response. This is normal and true for most human beings."[27]

Pushing through fear to activate faith and take next steps is where coaching can play a key role.

---

[27] Iyanla Vanzant, In the Meantime, (New York, Simon & Schuster, 1998), 254-255.

- What is keeping you stuck?
- What causes you to be afraid?
- What is the ultimate destination if you stay on the road you're on now?
- Why are you avoiding the inevitable?
- What would be the likely result if you could walk into your fear now?

Accept — Part of pressing on and pushing through the fear of change is accepting that things really are not currently working for you and/or your organization. Accepting this true reality and beginning to be totally honest will bring the true power for change and the innovative spirit. Often this acceptance and lifting the denial wrapped around a situation cannot be done without a coach or another outside perspective. We have often heard the phrase, "One must get out of the forest to see the trees." All objectivity is often lost if we continue to stay isolated, disconnected from change, and away from honest feedback.

- What will it take to allow you to accept that change is needed?
- What does that change look like to you?
- What new skills, attitudes, and behavior are needed to start the change?
- What is the best version of yourself you can see now?

Community — The process of change and movement forward cannot be done alone. A healthy and balanced outside perspective is needed. A coach is going to enter a situation with an open mind. A good coach will have the attitude of

"What will I learn from this new situation and coaching environment today?" In the coaching process, the coach and the PBC (person being coached) are always learning. The coach will help the group see things more clearly and allow the group or person to think, reflect, and collaborate on new options and possibilities for moving into one's true purpose and positive change.

- What can I learn from others in this situation?
- What am I learning about myself in regard to my own attitude and beliefs?
- How does the feeling of community and connection help when facing change?

Evaluate/Explore — Pushing through the fear, accepting that change is needed and wanted, and beginning to articulate these findings with a coach opens the path for exploration and evaluation. One coach tells his clients, "You must give yourself permission to window shop." What a clever way to say, "Get out there! Try new things. Explore." This cycle of exploration and evaluation can be done in many different ways depending on the group or individual. It may require small, focused, disciplined steps because too much change too quickly will turn the boat upside down. Or, a huge shift or leap of faith may be exactly what is needed to start one's new adventure. Could it be time to step out of one boat and get into a new one?

- How do you begin to evaluate places to explore?
- What does your criteria include?
- What does exploration look like?

Leaders must then MAKE change.

Coaching to **MAKE** Change

- Movement
- Adjust
- Kinesis
- Evolve

Movement — One thing we definitely know as coaches, change requires movement and action. I have a good friend who is always saying, "Let's see a little less talk and a little more action." We look at each other and laugh. But, what a great reminder for all of us. Many of us cannot begin any movement until we F-A-C-E our reality and admit we are stuck or in some cases moving backwards.

- How do we know when we are stuck?
- Where does movement start?
- How do you know if we are moving in the right direction?

Adjust — As movement begins, many adjustments will be needed. Personal adjustments and group dynamics begin to change. A coach will begin to walk you and/or the group through these transitions, which will be much more difficult and powerful than one might think. These movements and adjustments will affect people differently. Some will experience great excitement and renewed interest and passion. Others will begin to "stick their feet in the sand" and say, "Hold on! I am not sure these changes need to happen".

- What happens when adjustments begin to turn into conflict?
- When is conflict good?
- What can be learned through resolution of conflict?

Kinesis — During the movement and adjustment phase it is important to start paying close attention to what is pulling you and the group? What is feeding the passion and excitement for change? What is causing a drain or a tendency to pull back to the way things were? Is fear and uncertainty beginning to creep in and be the saboteur? When you are at this place, think about what pulls you towards the Light (kinesis). Your true gifts and calling will fuel your passion and excitement, not drain it. One coach constantly says to his clients, "Go to things and places that make your baby kick!" Pregnant women often feel the kick of new life within them, bringing great hope, joy and even sometimes fearful excitement and new energy for the rest of the journey. Embracing this energy and movement towards the things, people, and places that fuel your passion will keep the momentum needed and it will be a lot more fun.

- What makes your "baby kick"?
- What have you done today that makes you proud?
- What does moving into purpose and passion look like?
- Who can you stand beside and be your very best?

Evolve — As the movement, adjustments and kinetic process begin you and/or your group will start the evolution of new ideas, beliefs, strategies and goals. This is an exciting place to be as old ideas and patterns begin to unravel and the integration of the old and the new begin to fuse together. This then allows you to embrace your new world with much more courage and clarity. This progression is a big hope builder. You finally get to a place where you may not be certain where you are going, but you are sure that you do not want to go back to the way things were. This is a powerful tipping point for change. You are at the point of no return. There is no turning back. This is to be celebrated.

- How do you know your changes are turning into greater things and evolving?
- What are the pulls that tug on you to return to your comfort zone?
- What fuels you to keep pressing on?

Once leaders have started to F-A-C-E and M-A-K-E change, we then carry on with the integration of old and new ideas to embrace the new vision and world into which they are preparing to walk. John Trent calls this incremental transformation two degree shifts in his book, *Heart Shifts*. He explains, "It's the small marks on our soul that will shape our lives."[28]

---

[28] John Trent, *Heart Shifts*, (Nashville, Tenn.: Broadman & Holman, 2004), 22.

Here are ways leaders EMBRACE change.

Coaching to **EMBRACE** Change

- Experiment
- Manage/Maintain
- Bridges/Barriers
- Rebuild
- Align
- Challenge
- Explode

Experiment — At this stage, you truly begin to experiment with your new skills, mindset and ideas. By now you have done some "window shopping",· agreed on some things that you want to try and agreed on some things that you do not want to try. You are not actually at the place where you know for certain what is going to work and what is not going to work, but enough exploration has been done that it is time to take some risks, next steps and experiment with some new ideas, programs, and events.

- What are you and/or your group willing to try?
- How do you know who tries what?
- How do you measure the success of your experiments?

Manage/maintain — As these experiments begin to take place, a coach will help the group determine who, what, when and where. Just as in one's personal journey and an organization need to discern what it needs to let go of to move into a better purpose-filled life.

- Who should manage what?
- What needs to be maintained? What needs to be birthed?
- What needs to go away or be terminated?

Bridges/Barriers — As you begin to make these decisions, you will discover that some will be extremely difficult. Many will struggle here and will not be willing to look at and weigh the costs. As you enter this phase, remember giving birth is often painful. Understand the need to explore ways to build bridges instead of barriers. Looking for the win/win in a situation will increase your chances drastically for success rather than constantly using your time and energy to work through obstacles and barriers.

- How would you define a barrier? Bridge?
- How do you build bridges instead of barriers?
- How do you define a win/win situation?
- Are you a bridge-builder or barrier?

Rebuild — As you experiment and manage bridges and barriers, it will be time to reflect and discuss how the rebuilding will look. There will definitely be many things to rebuild as this process forces you to decide what to keep, change and let go of to move into your future.

- How does one begin to rebuild? What pieces do you keep?
- What pieces do you let go of? What pieces to you keep, but remold?

Align — As you align your new choices and discoveries with your intentional actions, your new world begins to take shape and unfold. This will be exciting but will feel unfamiliar and uneasy at times. Walking into the unknown and the unfamiliar takes us all out of our comfort zones and thus the personal and group challenges continue.

- What does re-alignment look like for you?
- How do you celebrate your successes as re-alignments begin?
- How do you learn from where you have "missed the mark"?
- What are your challenges at this point?

Challenge — The challenge is part of the test for birthing the new. Personal conflicts will surface and decisions will need to be made. Anything worthwhile will require courage, discipline and perseverance. As pioneers of change and change management there will be many trials and tribulations. Jim Collins states, "Every good-to-great company embraced what we came to call the Stockdale Paradox: You must maintain unwavering faith that you can and will prevail in the end, regardless of the difficulties, AND at the same time have the discipline to confront the most brutal facts of your current reality, whatever they might be."[29]

- Will you and/or your organization simply slip back into that old familiar comfort zone and not change?
- How will everyone handle this challenge?

---

[29] Collins, 13.

- Who will succeed and who will fail?

Explode — As coaches, we have seen this time and time again. As you F-A-C-E, M-A-K-E and then E-M-B-R-A-C-E change, a new world takes shape. Programs, events, organizations and more importantly people explode into their potential, passions and true calling. The "gold in the making" comes forth. People and organizations then go places and do things they could have never planned or imagined in the first steps of facing one's fears.

- How do you keep walking into the new?
- How do you teach others what you have learned?
- How do you stay strong/focused to keep/maintain growth and change?

Soulful-leaders not only navigate the waters of change, but soulful-leaders initiate the momentum of persons and organizations to explore their depths, their desires and their hungers through powerful questions and personal reflections that enables them to FACE, MAKE and finally to EMBRACE change. How do soulful leaders differ from other leaders? They lead from the heart and the head. They ask powerful questions, rather than tell or make personal declarations. Soulful leaders coach. They do not command. They lead by example. They walk the talk.

Section III

The Influence of
Soulful-Leadership

(((•)))

CHAPTER IV:

Soulful-Leaders Put Heart into Managing Change

Making Shifts In Waves of Change: Tools that Transform

The exponential changes of our time call for more than leadership – these times call for soulful-leadership. The deep changes on our threshold call for leaders with deep souls – leaders with virtues of wisdom, integrity, discernment, hope, patience, perseverance, and intentionality. In these tough economic and challenging days soulful-leaders more often than not are learning to lead in times of crisis and learning to use and maximize what is "in the box" rather than just focusing "outside" or "beyond the box." We are providing soulful-leaders two valuable insights that will allow them to face the waves of change with clarity instead of compromise, discernment and discovery rather than dread; and faith instead of fear. Leadership in days of crisis focuses on what works, what sustains, what is personal and encourages flexibility and accessibility, according to James Morrison. [30]First, we will introduce you to a new lens through which to examine the

---

[30] James Morrison, "How to Manage a Crisis," The Independent (London), Jan. 22, 2009, http://www.independent.co.uk/student/postgraduate/postgraduate-study/how-to-manage-a-crisis-1479583.html.

pebbles of possible changes cast at us. Second, we will provide leaders a new toolkit for working with the changes that you decide you or your organization needs to encounter and resolve in your context. The ripple model is all about creating flexibility and personalization and sustaining momentum during times of change and challenge. This coach approach will give you insights and tools to work with your issues. It will allow you to enter the process from any angle you choose as you customize intentional responses to change.

The first part of this book has introduced you to basic concepts used in professional coaching. These are only basic concepts. The more you practice them, the more empowering and transformational they become for you and those you coach. The remainder of this book introduces a Ripple model and 7 key questions that serve as tools that transform and Make Shifts In Waves of Change. The tools are transformational because they create and deepen the influence and impact of leaders, families, organizations and churches.

Benefits of Soulful-Leadership

Let's look at ways leaders can help their organizations through change. The Ripple model (as seen on an adjacent page) serves as a new framework that serves as a new lens for coaching through change. The 7 key questions and other models in the book and the appendices form a coaching toolkit for the soulful-leader.

The Ripple Model is based on the image of a pebble being thrown in a pond creating waves of hope, direction, encouragement and inspiration for moving forward. There are six suggested entry points (where the conversation starts) for using this model. Understand that these entry points will likely not be sequential.

1. Openness to change
2. Learning to face the unfamiliar
3. Self-awareness/clarity
4. Creating forward movement that creates momentum
5. Commitment to forward movement and community; and
6. Moving beyond denial to face reality.

These elements of the Ripple model are simply suggestive of some of the probable ripples created by the pebbles of change being cast in the tranquility of one's life or organization.

- This model is primarily a framework for the coach to listen to the person being coached for entry points, disconnects and what's missing.
- Using this model the coach listens for internal or external shifts the person is facing.
- As these shifts are discussed, explained and clarified this will determine their focus, which is the first part of the FAST model.

The new lens of the Ripple model provides a new way of listening, learning, and assessing the situation. These new methods are part of the soulful-leader's new toolkit.

Other parts of the toolkit are resources, strategies, powerful questions for building ownership, understanding, support, and an expanded leadership base focused on moving the person or group forward in effectiveness and relevancy. The new toolkit helps new dreams come alive to move through change in a way that moves individuals from pain to purpose, from wandering to walking and organizations from maintenance to mission to capacity building.

The models and powerful coaching questions are designed to tap into the heart of the leader and the others in the organization in ways that transform not only the persons but also the families and organizations in which they are involved.

Tools for Aligning Life and Purpose

The soulful-leader's new toolkit includes avenues for aligning life and purpose in ways that deepen the influence and the impact that fuels the transformation:

- 7 powerful key coaching questions empower persons or organizations faced with change.

- Resources unpack the implications and strategies for the person or group being coached.

- Applications are created for the context based on the personal or organizational mission statement or purpose.

- The value of the Ripple model is that it provides a filter through which to listen and a lens through which to look at the real situation before you.

- The 7 key powerful questions provide ways to get others onboard, clarify their understanding, enlist new leaders and explore possible blind spots and organizational implications.

- We also provide in the soulful-leaders toolkit other coaching models. These will help the coach or the client retain focus. The models allow them to gain traction after getting stuck when faced with BARRIERS or find a need to build some BRIDGES.

- Coaching is not necessarily a linear process. The best coaching follows the issues of the person being coached. If a coach listens carefully, the person will reveal the next question he or she needs to be asked.

- The 7 key questions, the RIPPLE model, and the BARRIERS and BRIDGES models that will be introduced to you in the next chapters can be used in any order that best serves the person or group being coached. The reality that coaching is a non-linear leadership process is often the biggest challenge for most groups and leaders. It is more an art than science. However, if you are working with a linear thinker or group, these models can be shared with them in order to help them follow and engage the coaching process. Remember, great coaching follows the energy and learning style of the person being coached. You can do it – practice and use the Making Shifts In Waves of Change learning cards found in the appendices. Now let's look at the Ripple Model and the 7 powerful coaching questions. We will use these in the remainder of the book.

Ripple Model for Coaching Individuals & Organizations

Moving from Pain to Purpose

Moving from Wandering to Walking

Moving from Success to Significance

Moving from Chaos to Harmony

Moving from Maintenance to Mission to Capacity Building

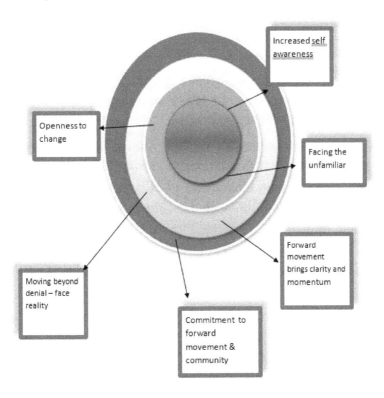

Possible Shifts and How to Make Them Happen

7 Keys for Making Shifts In Waves of Change

1. What are the shifts needed? Now?
2. What are the shifts about anyway?
3. Who needs to know about the shifts?
4. What do the dissenters/skeptics need to know?
5. What timing is needed in making these shifts?
6. Who can help us move forward now?
7. What is next?

Our previous book focused primarily on the church. *Reaching People Under 30 While Keeping People Over 60: Being Church for All Generations* (Chalice Press, 2015) has been very well received. It surfaces many leadership issues and challenges for church leaders. *Making Shifts In Waves of Change* seeks to provide leaders of all types of organizations and from all walks of life with an additional understanding of the coach approach to introducing and managing change. In effect, our previous book exemplified the value of the coach approach to a specific issue. This book explains how the coach approach can be used to deal with a wide range of issues regarding introducing and managing change and transition.

It is our belief that the best leaders for initiating and managing change are soulful-leaders that follow their hearts rather than just their heads. We discussed the distinctives of the soulful-leader in the previous chapter. Now, let's consider basic coaching questions for making needed shifts without making overwhelming waves.

When it comes to introducing and managing change many leaders are inexperienced, uninformed and/or unable to introduce effective change.

For example, in churches and other non-profit organizations, some key church families and leaders write checks on which the leader's family depends. Many pastors and leaders do not have the gifts or the calling to be a leader. They usually come to a church under job descriptions particularly crafted by church leaders to be sure the pastor will care for them, teach them, shepherd them, and manage programs for them. Rarely does a pastoral ministry description focus on leadership and introducing and managing change. That is usually the farthest thing from the minds of those on the minister search committee, but often it is the skill set the church needs most in order to move forward.

Today's rapidly changing culture has brought forth a deteriorating interest in the treasures of the church culture or even attending church. It's easy to see that today's churches or other organizations cannot avoid change. Some can deal with incremental change and survive and maybe even thrive. Most are in situations calling for systemic and radical change. For instance, many churches are filled with dedicated senior adults who staff programs, give tithes and design ministries. Similarly, many corporations have many tenured employees wanting to know what to do next. Increasingly the younger generation, particularly those who haven't grown up in church families, are not even thinking about church in their weekly activities. What's a church to do? How are pastors and churches to respond to the growing apathy of the culture while preserving those who are in the current membership and leadership pool? Thus, how can a church or any organization makes shifts without creating unnecessary waves of discontent?

Toolkit That Transforms Leaders and Organizations

Ken Blanchard, internationally respected author of the bestseller *The One Minute Manager* and countless other books, recently co-authored with Phil Hodges a modern day parable for the church – *The Most Loving Place in Town*. The book is a narrative of a pastor and congregation who are faced with change and the fears and apprehensions that often go with any change. In this book they summarize concepts of the 'soulful-leader' and powerful learnings about implementing change.

- All lasting change starts with clear vision and direction.
- The first thing people want to know when faced with change is information.
- The next thing they have are personal concerns – they want to know how the change will affect them.
- Once people's personal concerns are dealt with they want to know what the implementation plans are – what will happen first, second, third and so on.
- After these concerns have been dealt with, people are more open to hear about the benefits of the change.

- When implementing change, you don't have to do it all on your own.
- Developing a strategy to deal with fear and pride issues is important in any change effort."[31]

Another perspective regarding a soulful-leader and change from a colleague and friend is worth considering. John Trent writes about Heart Shifts and the importance and power of making two-degree shifts in behaviors, thinking, or maybe values in order to make meaningful and transforming change. He challenges us to work from our strengths rather than our weaknesses and to be intentional about making meaningful heart shifts. We agree. We affirm his beliefs about building "memorial markers" to celebrate the day you make heart shifts.[32] Such insights are key in helping leaders and organizations make shifts without making overwhelming waves.

There are keys for those who want to make shifts without making waves. These are framed in the form of powerful coaching questions because leaders who ask questions give the group being coached the power of the agenda. Decisions are made by understanding, and as awareness grows and decisions are made, the next steps are discovered and often owned. Building ownership and clarity and creating a landmark are critical. This takes time, patience and skill along with determination, reflection, and focus. The toolkit is

---

[31] Ken Blanchard and Phil Hodges. The Most Loving Place in Town, (Nashville, TN: Thomas Nelson, 2008) 123-124.
[32] John Trent, HeartShifts: The Two Degree Difference that will Change Your Heart, Your Home and Your Health, (Nashville, TN: Broadman and Holman), 91-99.

found in the timeliness of working through each of the following questions with key leaders, families and decision-makers. This must be done in a methodical, intentional and mindful manner, being sensitive to feelings while being clear about needed change. Transition is about the soft skills and feeling issues. Change is about moving the structure, core values and leadership forward to more effective service for a rapidly changing world. It's a balancing act but it is possible if you work the questions and build the ownership. (For more information on this subject, see *Managing Transitions* by William Bridges [Da Capo Press, 2003, 2nd Ed.]) People do not mind change nearly as much if they just understand why the change is being proposed. The process works even better when the people are allowed to design the changes they feel are needed at that time. Spiritual discernment is a key part of finding the right time and people, so pray and listen and observe "all things."

Powerful Coaching Questions

Build Clarity, Focus, and Ownership

Consider the following powerful coaching questions as tools for finding clarity and focus as you build ownership and understanding among all key decision-makers. We introduce you to the 7 powerful questions here and will apply them in the remaining chapters. Research tells us that if you can get about 25 to 30 percent to buy into a new idea, they can lead a culture shift in any church or organization. So often, the easiest groups to engage are those who are newcomers to the church and those who have children or grandchildren who are still in the community at large but are mostly inactive in the church. The newcomers can help create a new value and leadership model from the time they enter the fellowship. The other folks are looking for something meaningful that works to reach their loved ones. For church leaders we truly believe that God has a remnant in His church that sees the future and if led they are willing to help fund and create that dream. (The remnant is also discussed in *Spiritual Leadership in a Secular Age* [Chalice Press, 2005] and *Reaching People Under 30 While Keeping People Over 60.*

Key 1: What are the needed shifts?

This question opens up great conversations that immediately reveal what people value, what is working for them and what is not for them or those they love. Discovering together what shifts are needed for an organization to be more effective is key.

Key 2: What are the shifts about anyway?

Once the needed shifts are listed by key persons, you might then prioritize them by inviting the group to vote on the top five that would make the most difference and most impact in reaching persons they currently find unreached. After the five are identified, then list all the reasons these shifts are needed. Invite the group into this dialogue, and write these reasons for all to see on newsprint. This opens the door then for what others need to know to value the shifts as much as those in the dialogue.

Key 3: Who needs to know?

Hopefully, you already have most of the key leaders, decision-makers and key family members involved in the dialogue. Ask that group who else needs to know about this? Invite those who mention the names of others to approach them prayerfully and intentionally to raise their awareness of these issues and to get their feedback. Often those in the initial dialogue become legitimizers for others in the organization. Use that relationship wisely but intentionally.

Key 4: What do the dissenters need to know in order to buy into the proposed shift?

It is very unlikely that everyone in a group or in a church will agree with all the proposed changes. Do not let this stop you. Many churches and organizations that are dying let the fragile feelings of a few stop the forward progress for many. Give the dissenters an opportunity to voice their concerns. Ask them what they need to know to buy in. Let them know that you will be sure their opinions are shared with the entire decision-making groups. This is tough but essential.

Key 5: What timing is needed?

Timing is everything in change and transition. Change, in most cases, does not need to happen overnight. If the utilities and mortgages cannot be paid due to lack of participation, it may require radical change. Otherwise, patience, prayer and intentionality are needed. Craft a realistic timeline for making change happen. Invite others to respond to this with their insights and concerns. They often have ideas many have missed.

Key 6: Who can help move us forward?

Change and transition will not happen if it all depends on the clergy or just one leader or decision-making board. As more people in the pew buy into and have ownership of the new dream, a more effective and efficient new wave will emerge. Who are those you have discovered in the previous gatherings that have passion for the new? How can they help make this dream a reality?

This system sounds simple in some ways, but it works. Bathe it in prayer, reflection, and intentionality. It really is possible to make shifts without making overwhelming waves. Follow the keys, use more questions than declarations, and build ownership based on the heart and the relationships persons have with those who are disappointed or disenfranchised from the organization.

Key 7: What is next?

The coach approach is a forward-looking process that seeks to move organizations and leaders forward. In a way, it is a never-ending process. Soulful-leaders help their organizations to think about the immediate future as they consider the next step.

With these questions in mind, let's look at how the coach approach provides the framework through which individuals and organizations can grow and thrive.

$(((\bullet)))$

CHAPTER V:

Soulful-Leadership – Making Shifts That Matter In Individuals

Revolutionary Transformation Evolves from Mindful Shifts Involving Change and Transition

Now that we have looked at the distinctives of a soulful-leader and coach it's time to explore some models you can use as a soulful-leader to coach individuals through change and transition while maintaining as much attunement as possible. Finding harmony in many situations can be challenging and awkward at best, especially where there is resistance to, disconnection from and misunderstanding of the change taking place. In order to capture the harmonious nature of any situation, one first must be able to see and embrace the cause and effect of the decisions and progression for the shifts taking place. In these discoveries, the coach is looking for "the coachable moments." Harmony can be captured in the dialogue during these moments. Jane Creswell, master certified coach and author of Coaching for Excellence defines the coachable moment when a person is in a position to benefit from learning something new related to a specific focus area and is ready to take action on it.[33] People and organizations need to know why change is happening. Finding authentic coachable moments is a big part of this process.

Change and transition are two chief ingredients of most shifts that occur in people, teams and organizations. In this chapter we want to explore with you the coach approach to making shifts that matter in individuals.

Dictionary.com and William Bridge's book *Transitions* help us differentiate between change and transition.

Change is defined at dictionary.com in several ways. Among them are:

1. to make the form, nature, content, future course, etc., of (something) different from what it is or from what it would be if left alone.
2. to transform or convert to.
3. to substitute another or others for; exchange for something else, usually of the same kind.

According to the website transition is "movement, passage, or change from one position, state, stage, subject, concept, etc., to another; change."

In other words, change has to do with the hard side – the structure, organization, furniture etc. Transition is more the

---

[33] Creswell, 44.

soft side, the human element, the feelings, attitudes and emotions of change. This is often far easier than what Bridge's writings refer to as transition. Bridges states, "You find yourself coming back in new ways to old activities when you're in mindful transition."[34] He further declares, "The process of transformation is essentially a death and rebirth process rather than one of mechanical modification."

Change and transition are the keys for external and internal shifts that need to occur for soulful transformation in individuals and groups. This is usually not an easy and clearly defined process from the beginning. It is normally a bit chaotic. This process is much more organic and evolves and unfolds as one makes discoveries and has their "aha" moments of deeper understanding and clarity.[35]

Bridges states, "Chaos is not a mess, but rather it is the primal state of pure energy to which the person returns for every true beginning."[36] It is important for us to reframe our beliefs and thoughts around chaos to see it serves as a starting point for the opportunity for real transformation.

There will be times of uncertainty and doubt. Times of movement forward and times for reflection and sitting still will be required. This neutral zone, or what Iyanla Vanzant calls "in the meantime," is extremely important for saying goodbye to the old and having fertile soil for the new to begin. Bridges says another "reason for the gap between the old life

---

[34] Bridges, 8.
[35] Bridges, 119.
[36] Bridges, 119.

and the new life is that the process of disintegration and reintegration is the source of renewal."[37] One might even say that "the message is in the mess."

Shifts Involve 'in the Meantime' and Neutral Zone Strategies

In Vanzant's book "*In the Meantime*," she states, "There are hundreds of thousands of meantime scenarios that give depth and meaning to life. The meantime between jobs, the meantime between the argument and the reconciliation, between the separation and the divorce, between the test and the results. Each of these meantime experiences, although fraught with anxiety and stress that make them seem unbearable, are emotionally and spiritually profitable. A honeymoon is a meaningful meantime. Likewise, the period of labor preceding a birth is a meaningful but painful meantime. There are those meantimes which are immediately identifiable as being worthwhile and empowering, and there are those that wreak havoc on the soul. In the meantime, the clock stops and you are put on God's divine schedule."[38]

It is clear that the human side, the emotional side of change is often the most difficult and challenging. Change is more often than not an emotionally charged issue. People have emotional connections to places, times, events,

---

[37] Bridges, 120.
[38] Vanzant, 52.

traditions, rituals, and "the way we have always done it." Being sensitive to this and helping people to make these connections often dissolves emotional reactions or at least helps them find the root of the emotional reaction to change.

The following concentric model is a visual representation of the ripples often created through a coach approach that moves the individual or organization forward from a closed posture with an inward/self-centered focus to a focus with more of a systemic outward/missional focus. In today's world, we are moving from a missional focus (outward focus) to an incarnational focus (integrating head and heart focus), where persons must experience the new to fully embrace the new (the change or transitions encountered). As coaches, we work with many individuals who find themselves needing to move from pain to purpose, wandering to walking, from success to significance. Creating waves of hope and direction is the purpose of a soulful-leader and the essence of coaching through the ripple model. Explore how it might be used to create shifts in you.

Ripple Model
for Coaching Individuals

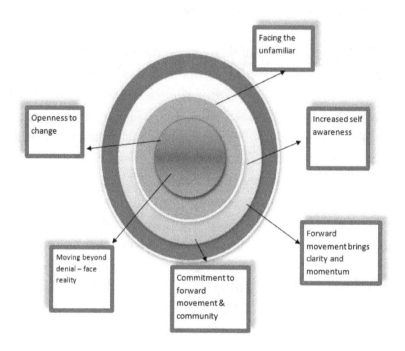

Possible Shifts and How to Make Them Happen

7 Keys for Making Shifts In Waves of Change

1. What are the shifts needed? Now?
2. What are the shifts about anyway?
3. Who needs to know about the shifts?
4. What do the dissenters/skeptics need to know?
5. What is the best description of the context of these shifts?

6. What timing is needed in making these shifts?
7. Who can help us move forward now?
8. What is next?

Framework for Using the Ripple Model

- People and organizations enter shifts from a variety of entry points and perspectives on life.
- Following the ripples from inward to outward focus offers a pathway to progress.
- Different grouping/ affinity groups follow essentially the same steps moving forward.
  - o Self-awareness/clarity
  - o Facing the unfamiliar
  - o Openness to change/shifts
  - o Moving beyond denial
  - o Forward movement brings clarity and momentum
  - o Commitment to forward movement and collaboration
- Effective shifts most often occur from the inside out.
- HARMONY model (see appendices) provides powerful coaching questions that move persons/ organizations forward regardless of where they might be when the coaching relationship begins.
- Progress occurs as persons/ organizations move forward from a purely self-focused perspective to an outward focused perspective.
- Often you have to change the behavior and then the feelings will follow.

- Clarifying limiting beliefs is often part of moving forward.
- Coaching is about discovering that which is already within and bringing it into light.

Adaptation of the Enles Scale

When coaching individuals around moving from pain to purpose, wandering to walking, or from success to significance it is important to realize that some external shifts often only occur after internal shifts have been made. Sometimes these internal shifts start on their own or begin with a bit of nudging from others and life experiences. However, in many situations, external factors and simply "life's hand" occur that demand our attention (without asking) and force us to focus on change. It is during these 'kairos moments' (divine appointments in the fertile soil of life lessons) - that test our character, integrity, soulfulness and willingness to embrace this transformational moment.

Examples of the Impact of the Coach Approach on Individuals

An example of an internal shift can be seen in a computer company executive who is extremely successful with his career and running his business unit but longs for more. His self-awareness seems to be high and he seems open. So he can be coached around options and forward movement. His financial success, corporate title, and responsibilities were simply no longer fulfilling. He is ready to move from success to significance. His passion and calling are to help lessen illiteracy around the world by getting books to those in need.

An example of an external shift is a smart, creative man who has had multiple successful jobs. He was laid off from his last job. He is uncertain of what he wants to do next. He is very capable of doing many different things. He may or may not have good self-awareness, and he may be in denial over job loss. If this is true, the coach might then ask, "What would be most helpful for you today?" or "What are your options?" If he gives himself permission to "window shop" a bit and explore new options around vocation and passions, he could experience an internal shift. He is still looking but eager to move from wandering to walking.

An illustration of moving from pain to purpose could be around leaving a painful relationship, leaving a job that one hates, a longing to spend more time with family, etc. Painful pinches can serve as the seedbed for tremendous growth and change. In all of these scenarios, one must say good-bye to certain people, places and things in order to say hello and welcome the new! One may reflect on the following questions as a self-assessment:

How did I get here? What will energize me? What brings me joy? Who is this affecting? Am I avoiding the inevitable? What describes the context of this situation now? What's desired in next 3 months? Do I love myself enough and others to face my fears and change?

Often the same life lessons keep coming our way until we have learned that particular lesson and are ready to move on toward higher self-actualization and deeper spiritual maturity.

Before we go into the 7 Keys, here are some things we want you to remember as an effective coach:

1. Entry points for your coaching conversations will be different – meet them (the PBC - Person Being Coached) where they are, not where you want them to be. Start where the client wants to start.
2. Make the client work hard to find their own self-discovery.
3. They set the agenda.
4. The PBC takes the initiative.
5. The conversations are about honesty and action; don't let them ramble and "beat around the bush."
6. Coach them through their barriers
7. Coach them to move their blocks.
8. Find the coachable moments (remember this brings the harmony to life!)
9. Listen for disconnects and blind spots – what is not being said.
10. Encourage and celebrate their learnings.
11. Create trust and hope. Open-ended questions create hope.

As individuals work on their desired changes in life, it is important to define and articulate exactly what is keeping them stuck. In other words what are the barriers that need to be labeled, understood and removed for one to have movement forward and ignite one's true potential.

A coaching model that might help is Timothy Gallwey's Realizing Potential model:

$$P = p - i$$

Performance = potential - interference[39] (barriers)

When using Gallwey's model, it is often best to work from the end to the beginning. In other words, consider first the interference and how it might be keeping one from reaching his or her potential. When that interference is lessened, performance is increased.

The things causing the interference are barriers to the desired outcome the person being coached is seeking.

The following BARRIERS acrostic is a helpful and easy way to help you as a leader and/or coach to navigate individuals from being stuck to unstuck. The coach needs to listen for barriers. Barriers could manifest as a false belief system, attitude, or saboteur. It could be someone's voice that they keep hearing that is telling them they are not good enough, smart enough, or adventurous enough. It could be fear. Shame. Addiction. Learning to unlearn these things that are keeping us stuck and relearning new ways that are good for us that push us forward to a better place can be extremely challenging. It is usually the internal blocks (i.e. personal thoughts and emotions) that are attracting the unhealthy

---

[39] W. Timothy Gallwey, The Inner Game of Work, (New York: Random House, 2001), 28

external blocks (i.e. the expressions of old patterns). Denial can be a coping mechanism for all of us at certain times in our lives but is not meant to be used long-term. It only keeps us stuck because we are not allowing the truth to enter in and birth our true self. Secrets, hiding things, and denial can be powerful blocks to one's forward movement. Denial keeps our false self strong and alive. Our false self does not want us to acknowledge our blocks, much less remove them and start using healthier coping skills and entering an authentic life. These internal issues often need an external person who is willing to mirror them for the PBC. Who needs to know about these struggles so they might be trusted enough to walk with you through the ripples from pain to purpose?

Clarifying BARRIERS

Coach Around **BARRIERS**
Bullet Proof
Avoidance
Resistance
Roadblocks
Impulse
Ego
Resentment
Sabotage

B — Barriers/Bullet proof – (Remember that the ripple model framework suggests lack of clarity/self-awareness, unwillingness to face the unfamiliar, and moving from denial might be areas in which to do some coaching.)

Difficult times test our character, our determination and willingness to change and become better. Moving forward toward health, wholeness, happiness and better decision-making requires us to look at what is keeping us stuck. One may reflect on these questions:

- What is in the way?
- What is blocking your path?
- Is it something external? Like a huge boulder in the road?
- Or is it something internal that is blocking our growth?

A — Avoidance

To illustrate avoidance and moving from pain to purpose, let me share this experience with you.

I (Randy)had a conversation with a dear friend one day. The friend is currently in a painful place. She called in sick to work because she needed what I call a "Me Day"- A time to relax, reflect and nurture one's soul. As we were talking, she said, "How did I get here? What have I done to get me to this place?" I asked her what she meant and what was going on. She had recently broken up with her boyfriend again. She believes that they do not have a future together. They have had an off/on relationship for years and have really had a difficult time cutting the ties. So, she has acknowledged here she is again in a situation that she has been in before; the pain of getting out and leaving the old is extremely difficult. The fear of being alone is overwhelming, and the fear of thinking of the dating world again and meeting new people starting all over is even more frightening and depressing.

We all seem to want to jump past the pain of the breakup and simply get into a new relationship where the euphoria and newness fill us up with joy and connection. But my friend is smarter now and has a bit more understanding of her decisions. She is beginning to notice some trends in the characteristics and qualities of the guys she dates and appears to be attracted to. Looking into her heart and inner self is scary for her because she said, "I am afraid of what I am going to find." I understand, and we talked about that a bit, but not too much. She was getting to the point where she did not want to talk about it anymore. Feelings and fears were starting to surface. We need time to explore, digest, reflect, uncover, change, and then act on our new learnings to break those unhealthy blocks that keep us stuck or attracting people that are unhealthy for us. I encouraged her to keep searching and to not be afraid at looking internally. My experience is that this cannot be done alone because we need the objectivity and trust of others. We also need a safe environment to do this important work. In a coaching conversation, you might want to explore:

- How do you know if a relationship should be terminated?
- How will you know if new healthy boundaries can be set? What is preventing you from leaving a relationship?
- What is preventing you from leaving a job that you have acknowledged as being a block in your life?

R — Resistance

Our resistance can be certain circumstances, viewpoints and/or fear of change. Perhaps there are lessons to be learned around our judgments, opinions, and abilities or inabilities to accept the diversities in today's world. Resistance is more emotional. For example, have you ever met someone who always has to be right? They must always win. It becomes a struggle for power. If they lose or don't get their way, they get upset and irritable. We all know that no one is 100 percent right all the time. Coaching is a powerful tool to move persons through their resistance.

Coaches may ask:

- What are your barriers that keep you in pain?
- What are you afraid of?
- What are you ashamed of?
- What are your triggers that set you off?

What makes your defense system kick in, and you become bullet-proof? This is usually a clear sign that this is the area that needs exploration and focus.

R — Roadblocks

Our blocks that keep us stuck could be people. Blocks could also be places, circumstances and/or things. A coach might ask:

- What is pulling you backward and keeping you stuck?

- What support do you have around you that nurtures the new dreams?

I — Impulse

Impulse is defined by dictionary.com as

A sudden wish or urge that prompts an unpremeditated act or feeling; an abrupt inclination. A motivating force or tendency: "Respect for the liberty of others is not a natural impulse in most men," — Bertrand Russell from dictionary.com.[40]

Unhealthy impulses cause us to say and do things that we regret and wish we could take back. Slowing down and taking time to work on ourselves is challenging at best. I just had a client thank me the other day for our time on the phone. I asked her what she meant by her statement. She stated that in her hectic life, she looked forward to the time on the phone with me to slow down and get to the core of life. She stated her coaching time served as a sacred place and time to block out the noise of life and hear the spirit of her inner voice.

A good coach needs to be fully present with the client and even mirror their energy or offer challenges to them that might go against their norm in order to create space for them to think, feel or learn. Here is such a case where a person who

---

[40] Dictionary.com, s.v. "impulse," http://dictionary.reference.com/browse/impulse (accessed Feb. 26, 2009).

is impulsive needs the coach to challenge them to stop – at least slow down and reflect.

Some reflective questions might include:
- What do I hear when I"m quiet?
- What's going on in the stillness?
- What keeps me busy?

E — Ego

Wayne Dyer is another inspirational writer and speaker that I (Randy) follow. He once said that the Ego is simply "Edging God out."[41]

Ego feeds the false self. It does not want to be wrong. Ego often feeds our greed and materialistic attitudes. Oftenour false self has no logic and rational thinking. Our false self is our aberrant behavior, our addictions, and dysfunctions that lead us to pain and unfulfillment. The false self wants to keep you stuck, unhappy and away from your true calling and destiny. And the false self will win unless we realize these are blocks that keep us from our true self. These blocks can be broken down and defeated by understanding the thoughts and feelings that take us to these behaviors in the first place.

Consider this coaching question:
- Where are some places you currently go that feeds your false self?

---

[41] Wayne Dyer, The Power of Intention, (Carlsbad, CA.: Hay House, 2004) 233ff

R — Resentment

Resentment is a barrier that manifests in our attitudes, belief systems, and unresolved feelings and emotions. Resentment is usually intentional. However, I have learned that for many persons, resentment is an emotional block that many use as an unhealthy coping skill. Many are in denial around resentment issues. So resentment remains quite intentional, but many are not conscious to their own behavior. I think one of the most interesting lessons I (Randy) have learned about my own blocks and triggers is that so many of mine were relational and wrapped around feelings, emotions, and a false belief system. Resentment and anger really did some work on me. Resentment is a big trigger for me. Resentment takes away all gratitude. Under my resentment were layers of hurt, betrayal, and grief. Resentment was my "I'll show them!" attitude and behavior. Anger can be a wonderful motivator to move forward, but resentment can be extremely ugly. I think we all know some folks that could use a good anger management course. Anger hurts others. Resentment, you simply hurt yourself.

Coaching assignments will often provide fuel to the client's agenda.

- Will you accept the challenge to sit down and start making a list, so you can begin to bring to life your awareness and acceptance of your blocks and toxins that feed your false self?

S — Sabotage

Getting to the truth and being 100 percent honest is very difficult and something that few of us do. We, unfortunately, for the most part are looking for a quick fix or a band-aid to a difficult problem and most of us are unwilling to do the depth of work required to let our true self shine and deaden our false self that is the saboteur. Pain and certain crisis in life, whether relational, professional, personal, or academic, can be used to get our attention and push us toward healthy or unhealthy behaviors. The decision to which way we go is up to one's clarity and understanding of self. We are at times, our own worst enemy. The false self wants nothing more than to defeat the true self and thus rob us of the destiny for which we were created.

This is a tough process that requires a lot of reflection and self-evaluation but is part of being a spiritual traveler (one who has spiritual thirsts but no necessarily formal connections with an institutional church or religion). And this individual journey makes us a bit different. Blocks and barriers have to be removed. To remove them, they must be understood. You must understand why and how the aberrant behavior got there in the first place. This moral self-inventory will require complete honesty and confession. It is ok to start this on your own, but I (Randy) learned that it takes the honesty and objectivity from others (a good coach) because at times we are not able to see ourselves and situations clearly through our own judgment and discernment.

Coaching questions to consider:

- How will you know if you are ready to do the work?

- What will move you into your fears?
- What are the benefits of uncovering your true self and moving into your destiny?

Another way of experiencing a transformation with a client is to utilize the seven key questions as a way of helping the client explore needed shifts:

Applying the Seven Key Questions

Key Question 1: What are the needed shifts?

The coach can listen for possible needed shifts about which the client may or may not be clear. Most people are moving from pain to purpose after the heart-wrenching realization that things are not the way they want them to be. In an individual's life, this could be facing the brutal realities around relationships that need to change or be terminated, family dysfunctions, unhappiness in a job, etc. For a group or organization, this could be a loss of revenues, employee retention problems, lack of productivity, etc. Whatever the issues may be, moving from pain to purpose requires greater self-awareness and clarity. Often things, beliefs, and ideas need to shift. At times old ways of thinking must change into entirely new learnings and discoveries. How long this takes depends on our pain threshold, our depth of denial, our openness to change, and our willingness to accept the truth.

Since you are trying to get a handle on the coach approach, here's a possible application of the coach approach using the first key question. So for review and application, consider these clues for coaching individuals. Remember, you are not nor are you expected to be a therapist that untangles emotions or the past. You are a coach seeking to move the coachable individual forward. If they are not ready to go forward, refer them to a counselor or therapist.

There must be openness to change and willingness to shift in order for forward movement to occur. If the group or person is bullet-proof, oftentimes, more dialogue is needed, time away for deeper thought and reflection may be required, or additional time may be needed to allow the people the sacred time needed for digestion and processing. Big life changes and shifts have a major impact on our soul as we best navigate to live our destiny and tap into our true callings. At best, this is messy! In our experience, it is very messy, but the Spirit and soul work is most alive and effective in the activity and collaboration for change.

As one's openness begins to unfold, one can begin to gently move beyond denial. As denial loosens it's grip, some will become much more interested and willing to invest in change and explore options for new solutions.

Possible coaching questions for jumpstarting a coaching conversation might include:

- What needs to happen today?
- What will help make that happen?
- What will you do if this does not happen today?

Key 2: What are the shifts about anyway?

This first key – What shifts are needed now? — is important and may have different entry points in the ripple diagram based on the person's goals and understanding to where they are currently. If the person being coached appears to have good self-awareness and clarity, the process may quickly advance from the inner ripple of the chart. If the person simply states that they feel stuck and have no idea where to go next, the coach will spend as much time as needed to gain clarity in regards to where they are now and where they want to go. For example, a client may state, "I hate my job. It is so painful to wake up in the morning, get dressed, and get into the office. My job drains me. I want to find greater purpose and explore what is my true calling in life." Now, this kind of statement and realization is fertile soil to begin an exciting coaching conversation.

In this particular example, the shifts are fairly clear – the person being coached might simply not understand the need for the shifts in the first place. Or it could be the client wants to change around job and fulfillment in their work life. This realization is great and is to be celebrated, but can create a tremendous amount of stress. It is natural for someone to want to change jobs and/or careers, but many of us will start making excuses to stay stuck. Some declare, "I have had this job a long time and feel very comfortable here." Often, that is not a reason to stay but a reason to move on and shake things up a bit.

Another consideration, today's work climate may demand external shifts, and it may not be much about internal shifts

MAKING SHIFTS IN WAVES OF CHANGE | 95

first. With downsizing and the increase in the number of pink slips, one's pain can easily be job termination from cutbacks. Key question two is important because our decisions will have an effect on those around us. It may be your family system, friends, and/or colleagues. This is where you want to help the person being coached explore all areas and where the ripple model can help you coach through the PBC's questions/issues and move them forward with these or other appropriate coaching questions.

As the initial conversations begin, you will quickly begin to realize that change is needed. Things simply cannot stay the way they are. This insight is a big first step, but many will get stuck at this early starting point. For after the realization that change is needed, one must then begin to look at the next steps. The next steps will be very unfamiliar. The old way is not working. All they know is the old way. Looking at options for a new way will be un-nerving and create uneasiness. Facing the unfamiliar cannot be done alone. One will simply slip back into their old ways quickly and will lose objectivity towards movement forward.

Coaching questions may include:

- What is really going on?
- What are the pinches here?
- What are the resources needed to move forward?

As you begin to embrace these questions and more importantly, begin to embrace some honest answers, two things may happen:

- Openness to change and shifts.
- Person shuts down and becomes defensive.

Question two (What are the shifts about anyway?) helps the individual explore and face unfamiliar landscapes that will be uncomfortable and tiring in the beginning. Openness to new learnings and stepping beyond one's denial and fears play a key part in birthing the new. As one pushes through the unfamiliar; momentum, clarity, and collaboration from others will increase. The next issue for many then is the loneliness they feel when it comes to moving forward with new behaviors or attitudes. Or they may fear failure as they embark upon new horizons in life and career. Then the coach might ask questions related to key question 3.

Key Question 3 - Who needs to know?

This begins to introduce and utilize the coach approach to a deeper level as you move beyond the first two questions. Our true self (the person we are created to be) loves us, nurtures us and others. Our true self has the freedom and confidence to dance in front of the mirror, show vulnerability, and have an open mind and an open heart. Our true self does not sabotage our future. Our true self demonstrates mind, body, and soul integration. Our true self has head and heart integration. Our true self is not self-absorbed and short-focused. Keeping our true selves strong requires great intention and dedication. One of the best questions I have ever been asked by a coach is, "Who can you stand beside that allows you to be your very best?" Great question. I think of this often. At times, other's personal agendas and motives can get in the way of one's passion and success. We need to know who are the persons that can propel us forward to our hopes, dreams, and goals. Who are the persons that can help us overcome our blind spots and challenges? Who is the person(s) that plays the role of "tough love" in your life?

These internal issues often need an external person who is willing to mirror them for the person being coached. Who needs to know about these struggles so they might be trusted enough to walk with you through the ripples from pain to purpose? The forward movement comes when the person being coached can respond and embrace the following questions:

- Who can help you move forward?
- Who can help you walk into the unfamiliar?
- Who can help you explore new options and create new discoveries?

Key Question 4: What about the dissenters?

In many instances, there are some internal voices that seek to sidetrack or sabotage the shifts. Or it may be those persons you hang around that seek to side track you from being all you are created to be. It also can be people that clearly do not understand the change and transitions you are trying to make. Sometimes they are not intentionally trying to stop you; other times they are so they can remain in their comfort zone or preserve their personal agendas.

- What's keeping you stuck?

- Who is keeping you stuck?

Key Question 5: What timing is needed to make these shifts?

The element of timing has to do with the coach and the person being coached. Here the coach looks for the coachable moments when the PBC is ripe for good coaching around a particular shift.

There is a great John Mayer song where he states, "I'm never really ready, I'm in repair, I'm not together, but I'm getting there."[42] The song articulates the journey, the process, being imperfect and accepting that this is part of the human condition.

We must accept that this is a journey — a life that will have failed relationships, career transitions, and great losses but also great victories and accomplishments. It is living by the lessons learned that move us to greater understanding, clarity, freedom, and fulfillment.

Coaching questions to consider:

- Where are you in your journey?
- Where do you want to be in 6 months? A year?
- What is the next step you are willing to take now?
- On a scale of 1 (unfulfilled) to 10 (very fulfilled) how would you describe where you are now?

---

[42] (John Mayer, Continuum CD, 2006 Aware Records LLC)

Key Question 6: Who Can Help Us Move Forward?

The reality is that, at times it can be very clear that people are blocks that keep us stagnant. At other times it can be much more subtle. But also it is important to know and embrace those who can move us forward. Peer pressure, at any age, is extremely strong in our world today. Children are being pressured into sex, drugs, and unhealthy behavior at alarming younger and younger ages.

Who are the cheerleaders for your new dream?
This powerful question can help you discover who can help you move forward.

People blocking our true selves can be the abusive caretakers in our lives. The abusive father or mother in a family system can cause a great deal of harm to one's self-confidence and self-esteem. This can be physical abuse, verbal abuse, emotional abuse, passive-aggressive behavior, etc. Many of us today have unresolved blocks that allow the cycle of dysfunction to be passed on and on throughout our family systems from grandparent to parent to child to grandchild. These issues trickle into our place of work, and then there is a new level of dysfunction created in the workplace with your teams and committees. For a true authentic change, the cycle must stop somewhere. Our blocks, toxins, and unhealthy coping skills are learned behaviors. They simply manifest in all of us in different ways. We all have our "Achilles heel" in life to deal with. This helps to keep us humble. I admire the saying I once saw on a T-shirt in Boston — "Be humble or be humbled!" Humility and surrender are important spiritual lessons in life that should be integrated into all areas of our lives.

Acknowledging that certain people and/or relationships may be a barrier for you can be extremely painful. We have all heard of extremely sad stories where the abused daughter will not admit that her mother or father is being abusive. The daughter cannot imagine telling someone what is really happening for these are her parents that love her and they don't really mean to do the horrible things that they do. We hear these conversations all the time in the coffee shop, the grocery store, the dog park, and on television. We have also all heard these statements around married couples and people dating, "Why does she stay with him? He treats her so badly. Why can't she see that he cheats on her and really doesn't love her? She would be so much better off if she could leave him."

Sometimes those that can help are authors of books who share similar journeys with you. One of my favorites is Terrence Gorski. He states, "If you came from a dysfunctional family, there are two very good reasons you may have trouble getting love right. The first is that dysfunctional relationships are contagious: Children catch them from their parents because they learn by doing what their parents do. If your parents were practitioners of destructive intimacy, that is all they were able to teach you. ... The second reason you are liable to have relationship problems is that dysfunctional families fail to provide their children with the emotional, intellectual, and communication skills necessary for healthy relationships. How can you drive a car safely without learning driving skills? You can't." [43]

Coaching around these issues can be effective if the person is ready to move forward and be coached. There is a coaching readiness factor that must be assessed. If the person is not able to move forward and appears tangled in their past, this is a good sign that counseling is really needed around these delicate issues and not coaching. Jane Creswell states, "The primary difference between coaching and other types of personal help is again related to who is viewed as the expert. Just as in athletic coaching, in mentoring, consulting, and counseling, the person offering the service is clearly the expert. In business coaching, the PBC is the expert. The coach is simply a guide to help the PBC keep growing, reaching goals, and achieving his or her potential".[44] (Current research is suggesting that personal therapy and coaching really complement each other. Coaching is being used as a powerful tool in some therapeutic sessions now with clinical professionals such as http://harvardcoaching.org/ with McLean Hospital and Harvard Medical School in MA.)

Coaching questions to consider:

- Who are the people in your life that erode your self-esteem and self-confidence?
- How do they prevent you from moving forward?

---

[43] Terence T. Gorski, Getting Love Right, Learning the Choices of Healthy Intimacy, (New York: Simon and Schuster, 1993), 33-35.
[44] Creswell, 14

- What things are you willing to give up to move forward?
- What are you not willing to give up no matter the degree of pain they cause?
- Who can move you forward?

For some the process of owning who keeps you stuck is essential in raising their awareness and encouraging them to open doors for those who can move them forward.

Key Question 7: What is next for you?

For me (Randy), "Taking off my tap shoes" was the next step. This is a phrase that I have used for years. I have never taken a dance class, nor do I own a pair of tap shoes, but I love all kinds of dance and think of the image of a professional tap dancer performing. They can really move at times, tapping faster and faster and faster. It is exhilarating to watch! This can be symbolic to my life, and I am certain for many others as well as we continue to be stuck in the cycle of our business and busyness. When do we have time to truly be alone to reflect? For after a great amount of reflection, we then need to move into action to change things that need to be changed. And this takes more time!

Ingrid Bacci says, "If you are afraid of being alone, you are dependent on others for your sense of self, and if you are dependent on others, you block your receptivity to inner guidance. Being willing to be alone involves being willing to be different, to have commitments and values that don't blend with any crowd."[45]

Staying busy was a barrier and coping mechanism for me. To stay so busy, never left me any time to look at myself and even begin to face my demons. This kept me in the cycle of quick knee-jerk reactions with little or no thought to my problems which in return put me in many uncomfortable situations. I can remember the first time I got home and did not turn on the TV, radio, or computer. I challenged myself to simply put everything down; the briefcase, the laptop, the cell phone, and the bundle of mail/bills. I sat on my couch and wanted to sit quietly for 15 minutes. I could not do it! My heart was racing, and my anxiety was building by the second. I had so many things I needed to do; bills to pay, people to call, a workout at the gym, etc. All things that truly could wait.

The first time I attempted to have my "downtime," I made it about 10 minutes before I jumped up, turned on the TV and computer, and jumped back into my life. Oh, the relief of being busy and getting back on the treadmill of my busyness to run from my problems and issues. The problem: that was not a long-term solution for me because as we continue to hide behind our unhealthy coping skills, our internal longing for clarity and our hunger for greater peace and purpose keeps tugging at us. And it will tug more and more until it gets our attention. I don't think I fit the category of a true workaholic

---

[45] www.thedailyguru.com, The Daily Guru, spiritual messages.

because my busyness could be centered around any project, not just work.

Gary Zukav states, "The pains and distresses and violences that you experience can be considered signposts along the path you have chosen. If you have chosen the path of learning through jealousy, for example, you will experience anxiety and fear of loss of what you think you cannot live without because these experiences are part of the path of learning through jealousy. If you choose the path of learning through anger, you will experience rejection and violence; if you choose the path of love, you will experience being loved by others, and so on, because the choice of a particular path is also the choice of particular types of experiences."[46]

Coaching questions to consider:

- How do you make time for more "downtime"?
- What scares you about having time alone?
- What emotions surface while you sit in silence?
- What do you hear in your silence?
- What happens when the activity/noise stops?
- What are your next steps?

As a coach, consider where you and the person(s) you are coaching are in the ripple model. Think about how the BARRIERS acrostic applies to your life. Ask yourself and the PBC (person being coached) the 7 key questions. When you're dealing with people who are going through the calm or

---

[46] Gary Zukav The Seat of the Soul, (New York: Simon and Schuster, 1990), 247.

overwhelming waves of change, remember the models, assessments and questions. These questions become tools of transformation in times and change and transition.

$((\bullet))$

CHAPTER VI:

Making Shifts That Matter in Institutions/Organizations

Soulful-leadership, whether you are dealing with families, individuals, churches, judicatories, or businesses, seeks to listen to those involved, discern collaboratively the next steps for the organization, and enlists the energies and resources of others to make the new dream and next steps become a reality. Coaching is a powerful tool to make this happen in a timely, efficient, and effective manner that honors the values of the past and co-creates an agenda that will move leaders, organizations, and dreams forward.

We have previously dealt with the coaching model when working with individuals. Chapter 5 is written from the ripple model and the BARRIER model, allowing you to see how coaching individuals can begin with their story, their awareness, or the lack thereof. While these same models and approaches might also be feasible and effective working with organizations, chapter 6 is written around the 7 key questions and coaching tools for building BRIDGES between members of the organization or group faced with change. Understand that all models and approaches are possible tools for working in some or all situations. Determining the best model and approach for a given coaching relationship depends on the coach's skill and the client's openness and learning style.

Working with teams, groups, organizations, businesses, churches or judicatories calls for basically the same skill set and often uses some of the same principles and models we have introduced previously. However, there are some significant distinctions that must be considered and incorporated into effectively coaching more than one person.

Distinctive to Remember When Coaching Organizations

Coaching a group or organization utilizes the basics of coaching along with another level of skills including these:

- Listening at deeper levels to hear even what is not being said and paying attention to more than one person at a time.
- Inviting the group to establish their own ground rules for the coaching session. What is needed to insure effective decision making from this organization now? What are the non-negotiables for this discussion?
- Insuring that all voices "at the table" are heard.
- Finding and keeping focus for the organization and leadership team.
- Honoring the values of the organization the group wants to preserve and what the members need to let go of to be more effective in their marketplace.
- Honoring confidentiality as you work with the group as a whole or individuals in the group.
- Co-creating consensus through coaching.

- Capturing the data from the group's dialogue around the 7 keys so the group/organization can then see and make decisions. The group selects a recorder to capture the thoughts.
- Creating win/win scenarios whenever possible.
- Honoring different learning and communications styles of the group (i.e. some need visuals, others need dialogue, others need processing/reflective times).
- Remembering that coaching can require linear, cyclical or random approaches depending on the learning or workstyle of the group.

Most organizations – whether profit or non-profit, face changes on almost a daily basis. Many organizations wrestle to preserve heritage and values while customizing services to meet the needs and wishes of a changing demographic, economic base, cultural system, etc. Staying relevant, flexible, and real in a rapidly changing culture is a challenge at best for any organization. Coaching can and does help leaders and organizations customize and contextualize services. Coaches who work with organizations understand the ingredients of creating a coaching culture and the power of assessing readiness and coachability. Without readiness and openness to change no person or organization can experience healthy and transformational change.

Let's toss another pebble of change into the waters and look at a way of making shifts in waves of change in organizations and institutions. This model applies to profit and non-profit organizations, churches, judicatories, and denominations.

Assessing Coachability

First, how do you know that an organization or institution is coachable? This is a key question. Some organizations want a quick fix to a challenge. In reality, they need the expertise of a consultant. Here are some indicators that an organization will respond well to a coach approach to introducing and managing change:

- The leadership team that makes decisions is open to challenge, open to change, and eager to work with others to make it happen.
- Organizational members or employees are open to challenge, open to stretching, open to change (stepping outside their personal comfort zones), and eager to work with each other to make change happen.
- Core values of the organization are understood by key leadership or there is a willingness to define them.
- Willingness to expend energy to discover next steps and how each leader and member or employee can work to move the organization forward.
- Openness to collaboration with others and willingness to hear all sides of an issue before making a decision.
- Openness to establishing a timeline to implement whatever changes are discovered and decided upon.
- Key issues of coaching are likely to include but are not limited to the 7 key questions.

Often coaching a group, organization, or team brings unique challenges. Patrick Lencioni offers excellent tools for working with teams in The Five Dysfunctions of a Team.

[47]Jane Creswell offers some practical summary statements to guide the coach in working with dysfunctional teams.

- Observe the team and determine the dysfunction that seems to be holding up the team most;
- Ask questions in the coaching conversation that will help the members discover their dysfunction and shed light on the actions they need to take to improve their team dynamics. (i.e. If you see lack of trust: Ask, How often do you admit mistakes to each other? What would have to happen for you to feel safe admitting mistakes with your team?)[48]

Keep in mind that the framework in the ripple model includes: openness to change; facing reality; increasing awareness; learning to face the unfamiliar, a mutual commitment to forward movement and community and embracing a forward movement that will create clarity and momentum. Learning to hear or observe these issues becomes critical for creating waves of hope among the ripples of change.

Other distinctives of working with organizations involves probable work with teams. Patrick Lencioni's The Five Dysfunctions of a Team provides great insights for coaches seeking to identify the nature of the team they are invited to coach. Lencioni's model is built around identifying the five dysfunctions of a team:

---

[47] Patrick Lencioni, The Five Dysfunctions of a Team, San Francisco: Jossey-Bass, 2002)
[48] Creswell, 103

1. Absence of trust;
2. Fear of conflict;
3. Lack of commitment;
4. Avoidance of accountability;
5. Inattention to results.[49]

He goes on to provide indicators the coach would look and listen for that might suggest members of a team are exhibiting one or more of the dysfunctions.[50] Lencioni also provides a very helpful self-assessment that the team can use to self-assess their health or dysfunction. [51]

Now let's explore each area from a coach approach as the pebble of change hits the pond that ripples through an organization.

---

[49] Lencioni, pg. 188-193.
[50] Lencioni, pg. 197-220
[51] Lencioni, pg. 191-193

Ripple Model
for Coaching Organizations

Moving from Maintenance to Mission to Capacity Building

In Families; Teams; Profit and Non-Profit Organizations

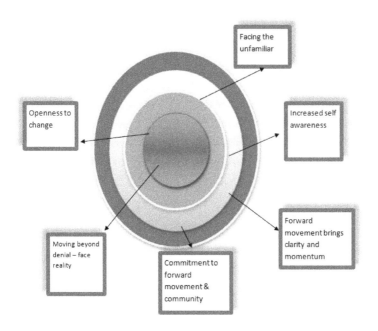

Possible Shifts and How to Make Them Happen

7 Keys for Making Shifts In Waves of Change

1. What are the shifts needed? Now?
2. What are the shifts about anyway?

3. Who needs to know about the shifts?
4. What do the dissenters/skeptics need to know?
5. What timing is needed in making these shifts?
6. Who can help us move forward now?
7. What is next?

Framework for Using the Ripple Model

- People and organizations enter shifts from a variety of entry points and perspectives on life.
- Following the ripples from inward to outward focus offers a pathway to progress.
- Different groupings/affinity groups follow essentially the same steps moving forward but not necessarily in the same order.
  - o Self-awareness/clarity
  - o Facing the unfamiliar
  - o Openness to change/shifts
  - o Moving beyond denial
  - o Forward movement brings clarity and momentum
  - o Commitment to forward movement and collaboration
- Effective shifts most often occur from the inside out.
- The HARMONY model (see appendices) provides powerful coaching questions that move persons/ organizations forward regardless of where they might be when the coaching relationship begins.
- Progress occurs as persons/organizations move forward from a purely self-focused perspective to an outward focused perspective looking for the coachable moments.

- Often you have to change the behaviors and then the feelings will follow.
- Clarifying limiting beliefs is often part of moving forward.
- Coaching is about discovering that which is already within and bringing it into light.
- Discoveries are most often made in community rather than isolation.

Let's look at a coaching scenario that's representative of the type of change issues faced by many organizations. A personnel search committee calls for coaching as they begin their assignment to seek new persons to fill vacated positions. Now, the overall goal is fairly simple. The committee needs to hire some new employees. Now, let's dive into the details. There are five members on the search committee. Two persons want to replace a person in the same position that was vacated. Two others want to tweak the position before the search begins. The fifth person wants to find the person then tweak the position. They want the coach to help them move forward. What's a coach to do?

The scenario is not unusual. You get five people in a room and often you have differing opinions, beliefs, values and attitudes. Not to mention that the skill level or interest of the persons involved will likely differ as well. If the group is open to exploration and willing to work toward consensus, a coach can help them focus and move forward. Consider this coaching model as a tool in this scenario:

Building BRIDGES

Building bridges is important when a group comes from different situations and is working to find unity of purpose and a common direction towards harmony because if you are not building bridges you are likely building barriers. (Note: While we used the BARRIERS model in chapter 5 with individuals and BRIDGES in chapter 6 for institutions these tools can be used in either coaching situation.)

Coach To Build **BRIDGES**

Belief Systems

Relationships

Intention

Discover

Gifts

Engagement

Summarize

B — Belief systems – Gaining clarity of what is really going on and what brings each committee member to their position is critically important. It's also important to discern the emotional landscape of those in the decision-making group. Beliefs often limit our perspective and impact our behavior, building bridges instead of barriers. Consider coach approaches like:

- Tell me more about your position regarding this assignment.
- What are your concerns about the issue at hand?

- What are your concerns about the position of others regarding this staffing issue?
- What do you need to know about their position?
- What is needed now?

R — Relationships — Coaches work to create a spirit of cooperation and discover what type of relationships already exist with those in the room. This often provides direction and clarity and helps the coach and each person understand the dynamics at work. (In other words, who are the friends, foes and family members?) So taking time to understand and build relationships, observing the group carefully, looking and listening for disconnects between what they say and how they behave will be helpful. Consider a coach approach like:

- What do you need the committee to know about you?
- What brings you to serve in this capacity now?
- Who are your heroes in life?
- What relational skills are important for leaders?

I — Intention — Discovering the intention of a group or individual is also important in a coaching scenario. A coach needs to discern the coachability of the group and of the individuals in the group. If the intention of one or more is to side track the group, bring a personal agenda to the group or sabotage the mission of the group that needs to be surfaced, acknowledged and dealt with appropriately.

- What would be the ideal situation here?

- What would be the best version of this job description/position?
- What would you like to change in our process?
- What would you like to change with this job description?
- What is driving your idea?
- What do we need to resolve today?

D — Discover — Sometimes a group simply needs to explore options together to move them forward. Limiting visions/ideas or beliefs often prevent persons or groups from seeing "outside, much less beyond the box." It can be a powerful dialogue to discuss what the group knows and then have them discuss what they don't know. Consider this coach approach:

- What are the possibilities here?
- Who are the persons might we talk with about these options?
- How can we discover the benefits/challenges of each option?
- What are the likely consequences if we do not look at other possibilities?
- Which of these options do you value most? (Prioritize the list individually and then as a group and compare results for a consensus direction.)
- How much time/energy are we ready to give to each of the top 3 options?

G — Gifts — Discovering the type of gifts/skills needed by a potential leader is critical. What gifts/skills are needed is a place for building consensus and finding a focus. Allowing one to use their true gifts and skills will unleash the true passion for the individual and group to excel. Consider this coach approach:

- What strengths are we looking for?
- What if we do not find the best skill set for this position?
- Which of these strengths are most important for this position?
- What might be the outcome if we do our assignment well?
- What if we miss the mark?

E — Engagement — Coaching is about moving people to action not just dialogue. Prior to this piece of coaching the coach needs to have worked hard to make certain every member of the committee has been heard and had the opportunity to respond to each other's responses to the previous explorations.

Consider this coach approach to move them to engagement:

- What are we ready to act on now?
- What is needed to make this a successful step now?
- Who will do what by when?
- What is still unresolved?
- What barriers still exist here?
- What do we need to do prior to the next meeting that can move us forward?

This movement forward may be incremental or it may be radical for the group's progress, but either is great. Working to find commonality among beliefs, limitations, and next steps is the goal here.

S — Summarize — Summary by the person/group being coached is critical to moving forward. Allowing the client to do the summary builds ownership and accountability. The coach needs to listen carefully as each summarizes and if there is a major disconnect or lingering evidence of sabotage the coach might need to ask permission to offer a challenge to the group that will help them move forward. It might be a homework assignment for reading, self reflection, or interviewing others. The group, of course, can accept, amend or deny the challenge. Consider this coach approach.

- Who can bottom line (i.e. succinctly summarize) discoveries made in this meeting?
- What are the top three things we decided?
- Which discovery made the most impact for you?
- What are our next steps now?
- What do you need now? (ask each person and the group as a whole)

Using the 7 Keys in Coaching

Key 1: What are the needed shifts?

After examining the ripple model, the coach will listen carefully to see where the group or individuals in the group might be entering this model. In fact, various people or teams in the organization may enter at different places. The coach and those being coached discern where they are and where they want to focus first. In order to know the needed shifts in a given situation the group must have a clear outlook on the goals they wish to accomplish. These goals do not have to be written in stone. They can definitely be altered and adjusted, but a good sense of where you want to go needs to be articulated and agreed upon. This is actually the easy part! The hard part: once you have some idea of where you want to go, you and the group must then decide how to get there and when.

Moving From Maintenance to Mission

Organizations typically find themselves either trying to move from a maintenance posture of day to day activity to a more progressive mission or moving from the desperation of finances and customer base to the hope of a more profitable future. The coach's role is to create some waves of hope amidst the realities of the organization. Such issues open the door for coaching and particularly with key question two:

Key 2: What are the shifts about anyway?

Taking the same scenario, let's explore the coach approach when working with this committee around the shifts they have previously identified utilizing the questions from key 1.

Factors that a coach should be tuned into as the committee or team seek to assess what the shifts are about anyway. Coaches also need to keep in their mind the HARMONY framework (see appendices) as a way of Making Shifts Without Making Waves.

Let's clarify the difference here between a team, committee approach and community approach. What are the distinctive of each type of group as they interact with transformational change? Generally speaking

Committee Approach	Team Approach	Community Approach
Focus on preserving the institution	Focus on collaboration and consensus in decision making	Focus on establishing community, belonging
Long term commitment called for	Short term commitment	Willing to show up when needed to accomplish community goals
Constitutionally driven (driven by governing documents more than current vision)	Relationship driven	Community driven
Institutional Concerns and Orientation	Need and Task-Oriented	Fellowship/Community Need Orientation

Clarity of the issues – the soulful-leader checks this out with the committee, team or community but also with each individual as you begin this next step of the change process.

- Personal agendas versus group agenda.
- Time line.
- Sense of urgency.
- What is your mission statement?
- What is value added? Passion around the issues – both passion of individual committee members and the passion of the group.
- Potential for sabotage or derailing the conversation.

Think again about the scenario raised earlier. The personnel search committee calls for coaching as they begin their assignment to seek new persons to fill vacated positions. Now, the overall goal is fairly simple. This committee needs to hire some new employees. Now, let's dive into the details. There are five members on the search committee. Two persons want to replace a person in the same position that was vacated. Two others want to tweak the position before the search begins. One of these persons wants a walk around type manager; the other person wants the position to be filled by someone who can raise money, do promotion and be a keynote speaker at community events. The fifth person wants to find the person and then tweak the position. (This committee member seems to already have a person in mind that they know and would like to tweak the position just for that person.) They want the coach to help them move forward. What's a coach to do?

Coaching skills, to draw from to move this committee forward with the new information that surfaced from the committee in previous coaching sessions might involve:

- Working toward consensus.
- What is resonating with you now?
- What are the top three issues we have discovered that need our attention today?
- How would you prioritize these issues in terms of importance to accomplishing your goals?
- How should we proceed now?
- What are the main tasks and duties of the open positions? Do you want these to change?

- They surface things like some wants one style of leadership and others want another style of leadership. How do we resolve this?
- Drilling down – (i.e. the coach drills to get clarity, focus and consensus from each person and group) Tension emerges, but resolution and clarity will bring great relief and direction.

The group identified as their top three issues: 1) Needed timeline for employment; 2) Differing thoughts about job description; 3) What will success look like in this situation?

- What are the disconnects you see here?
- How can we determine what's best for us now?
- What are the basic criteria for this position that are non-negotiable?
- What are the negotiables?
- How's your energy around this now?

Keeping them focused is a greater challenge with a group than with individuals and demands intense and skilled coaching.

- How we doing?
- What progress are we making here?
- What next steps are emerging?
- Moving them to action

Key 3: Who Needs to Know About The Shift?

Supporters and champions of the shifts and those who are skeptical about the change need to know. Getting all the needed leadership persons on board with the decisions is critical. It's not essential to have everyone embrace the change before you make the needed shifts. In fact, this is a key barrier many groups face — they want to get everyone in the organization on board before they do anything. That will likely never happen, but research tells us that the tipping point for making a change in an institutional culture takes about 20 to 25 percent of active membership. Then their family and friends or colleagues will follow those who are trusted and legitimize the new direction, and you pick up another 20 to 30 percent of persons, and the shift can be made. This points out the value of inviting some dissenters or skeptics into the group leading the change process. (See *Innovation of Diffusion* and *The Tipping Point* for additional information on this research.) When the skeptics get their concerns addressed and they become advocates, their shift generates shifts in others who trust their opinion and leadership.

Coaching questions might include:

- Who else shares your concerns?
- How can we hear their concerns?
- What do they need to know that we can now provide?
- Who is the best person(s) to share this information or conduct this interview?

Key 4: What do the dissenters/skeptics need to know?

This is a crucial question for the leadership team to determine and strategize how and when best to respond. Very often, those skeptics raise questions or issues that are valuable insights for the leadership team. Often even the leadership team can have a blind spot when it comes to change, or the members of the team may be driven more by their personal agendas rather than what is best for the organization. Some coaching questions to get at this includes:

- Who are the skeptics?
- What are their top three concerns?
- If we can only address two of the three concerns which are most important to them?
- What is driving their need to know?
- What does their concern say that we (leadership team) need to hear now?

An example of this came for me when "Mr. B," a declared dissenter to policy and procedural changes in our church had an epiphany that shifted his opinion, and his influence and impact help shift things so the congregation I was serving could move forward. One man, and his wife, gained a clearer understanding of the situation as a result of hours of conversation, reflection, and prayer. This insight was announced and the changes and transitions needed to move the organization forward began as ripples in a lake. Mr. and Mrs. B understood, and voiced their support, their family came on board, then their friends and their family's friends and the shifts happened!

Key 5: What timing is needed?

Timing is significant when introducing and managing change. Discerning the best time to have certain dialogues with certain persons can make or break the power of the moment. Determining coachability is one thing, but determining the right time for this conversation is another thing.

- What are the indicators of the right time?
- Who needs to know?
- When do they need to know?
- How much does each person need to know?

Key 6: Who can help move us forward now?

Change needs cheerleaders, champions, dissenters, and advocates. Influence of others makes a significant impact when introducing and managing change. Coaching questions might include:

- Who are the influential persons in the group or organization you are seeking to impact with change?
- Who are the legitimizers in the organization?
- Who can help open new doors of opportunity?
- Who are the persons that can make the most impact on the most persons now?
- What support do they need now?

Key 7: What is next?

Coaching seeks to move organizations and leaders forward. Determining what is appropriate and when is critical in forward movement. Inviting the leadership team, and others who have joined the change process, to help determine what is next for the organization builds ownership, establishes deepening trust and creates an atmosphere of hope, anticipation and possibilities.

Coaching questions might include:

- What needs to be first?
- What will make the most impact now?
- What are the benefits of this shift for the organization?
- What are the possibilities now for our organization?
- What do you need from the organization now?
- What does the organization need from you now?
- What are you willing to do now to improve the organization's effectiveness and value?

The 7 keys are a standard toolkit for a soulful-leader who uses coaching to introduce and manage change. These key questions unlock key issues, values, timelines and a focus that ensures forward movement even amidst diversity. These 7 key questions are applicable to working with individuals, families, businesses, profit and non-profit organizations. A successful coaching experience hinges on three key factors:

1) Coachability of the person or organization in question;
2) Determination of everyone involved to move forward; and
3) Willingness to face the unfamiliar and walk into the new (as decided by the group).

Making Shifts In Waves of Change is a prevalent challenge for families, businesses, individuals and organizations of all sizes, found in almost all contexts. This reality hinges on the rapid pace of change being generated in our increasingly pluralistic culture that is driven in large part by the fast pace and exponential changes brought about by technology. Natalie Gillam puts it this way: "In a world where power is in information and innovation, it is vital that leaders encourage innovation and new ideas and that they value diverse thinking within their team. Without this an organization risks being left behind."[52]

Gilliam continues by declaring that "providing enough opportunities for listening and challenging the status quo is vital, as without these forums it is difficult for people not to become consumed in day-to-day activities and tasks, never engaging with the debate."[53]

---

[52] Natalie Gillam, "Be a Successful Business Leader Even in Tough Times," Emirates Business24/7 , Nov. 28, 2008, http://www.business24-7.ae/Articles/2008/11/Pages/11282008_64e116def112417da687f13107b9715d.aspx
[53] Ibid.

Return on Investment for Individual and Organizations

In these challenging days, every business is seeking to get the best return on investments. "According to a recent Sales Performance International survey of sales managers at 134 different companies, inaccurate forecasting had become a big problem for them. In the survey, sales managers cited poor forecasting more often (54 percent) than either declining revenue (49 percent) or inadequate coaching (34 percent)."

Achieving maximum return on investment seems to correlate with these three criteria "Most sales managers strive to meet three success criteria:

1. Make the revenue numbers.
2. Forecast sales revenue accurately.
3. Coach and develop the right team of people to get the job done.[54]

Too many companies and too many sales managers hire experienced salespeople, believing they know how to sell. However, even the very best salespeople need ongoing coaching, mentoring, and training to maintain their peak performance."[55]

---

[54] Keith M. Eades,The New Solution Selling, (New York: McGraw-Hill, 2004), 244.
[55] Eades, 256

In an article titled *"Spotlight on Coaching As a Leadership Development Activity"*[56] in the Ottawa Business Journal, Craig Dowden says "the most effective coaching relationships are client-driven, because what works for the coach may not work for the client (eg., coachee) in his or her situation. Thus the role of the coach is to ask the right questions to get the coachee to think differently about certain challenges they are facing rather than 'telling them what to do' or producing an off-the-shelf solution. Considerable research and experience has shown that engaging clients as part of the solution maximizes the possibility of their long-term success."

Dowden discusses four ways coaching is valuable to an organization.

a) *Opportunity to engage in fire prevention versus fire fighting.* Dowden says modern managers are under tremendous pressure and, "rarely get the opportunity to engage in an important aspect of their role, which is to think strategically." Many have noted that working with a coach "requires them to set time aside every week, or month, to discuss and think about the 'bigger issues' that are affecting their job."

---

[56] Craig Dowden, "Spotlight On Coaching As A Leadership Development Activity - Some Issues To Consider," Ottawa Business Journal, Nov. 28, 2008, http://archive.ottawabusinessjournal.com/archive_detail.php?archiveFile=2008/November/28/OBJ-BusinessMatters18/25709.xml&start=0&numPer=20&keyword=craig+dowden&sectionSearch=&begindate=1%2F1%2F1999&enddate=12%2F31%2F2009&authorSearch=&IncludeStories=1&pubsection=&page=&IncludePages=1&IncludeImages=1&mode=allwords&archive_pubname=OBJ-Web%0A%09%09

b) *Opportunity to brainstorm* – Managers often feel isolated, Dowden says. A coach can serve as a "trusted advisor" who helps sort through issues and acts as a "sounding board." This "is enormously valuable to the executive, both in terms of raising their self-awareness as well as finding the answers they need by 'talking through' their challenges."

c) *Opportunity for honest feedback* – Dowden points out that as individuals ascend the corporate ladder, they often receive less open and honest feedback. "Bringing in an external coach allows a mechanism for gathering this information to occur, such as via 360-degree feedback or psychometric/personality assessment," he says.

d) *What got you here won't get you there* – Top performing employees often "struggle mightily when they are thrust into a management role," Dowden says. Coaching plays a crucial role in helping develop leadership and people management skills, through increasing the manager's own self-awareness and helping them recognize that their view of the world may not be shared by others. "Thus, coaching supports the manager in leveraging the strengths of the organizational talent pool by engaging with each individual team member in a way that matches his or her needs," he says.

Dowden says that once an organization has decided to use a coach, it should determine its goals for the process, decide who is going to receive the coaching and find well-credentialed coaches.

Dowden continues by explaining, "Once an organization has decided that management coaching is right for them, where do they begin? Indeed, there are several crucial questions and issues that need to be addressed to maximize the opportunity for a successful coaching relationship. Here is a partial list of things to consider:

a) *Clarity of purpose* – Essentially, what is the goal of the coaching assignment for your organization? Often, many organizations (and coaches) get involved without truly understanding these expectations. Therefore, it is essential, or highly recommended, to work out an 'Accountability Contract' that outlines the roles that each party (e.g., coach, client, and corporate client) will play in this engagement. Recent research by the American Management Association (AMA, 2008) www.amanet.org showed that the clearer the reason a company had for embarking on a coaching program, the better the programmatic results.

b) *Who receives it?* According to a survey conducted by the AMA, the three most common groups to receive coaching include high potential employees, problem performers and executives. However, as with any leadership development activity, it is important to consider the message being sent to the rest of the organization if coaching is only being provided to one of these groups. For example, if coaching is only given to the top performers, this may be quite de-motivating for the rest of the company. Conversely, if it is only used to address 'problem employees,' it may be viewed quite negatively, and may carry a stigma that will be difficult to discard at a later date. Thus, the potential implications of utilizing this type of development activity on the corporate culture should be considered before moving forward.

c) *Credentials?* Coaching is one of the fastest growing professions in the world today. Everything and everyone seem to be in the midst of transition and change on one or more levels in career, family, education, finances. Finding a coach with proper credentials is increasingly important. The International Coach Federation www.coachfederation.org is the lead credentialing body accepted in most professional circles. However, when faced with an endless selection of seemingly strong candidates, what are the most important differentiators? To answer this question, I would refer the reader to the AMA global study on coaching (http://www.amanet.org). In their review, they picked 10 common 'selection criteria' for coaches and examined whether they had a significant impact on future market performance. Some of the criteria that they looked at included coaching certifications, accreditation, recommendations from a trusted source, university degrees in a related field, etc. Of these, only THREE had a significant statistical relationship with market performance:

1) Business experience
2) Consulting experience and

3) Having a Ph.D.

Although the first two have been widely viewed as being important in the past, the last criteria may seem somewhat surprising. However, as mentioned by the study authors, 'one possible reason for this is that Ph.D.s bring a level of expertise to a field that has very low barriers to entry' (pg. 24). Based on the above, it appears that these three factors are the most important when it comes to maximizing the ROI of coaching in terms of the bottom line.

Dowden concludes that coaching can tremendously benefit an organization. "In closing," he says, "developing people is the most important thing an organization can do, and finding effective and empowering ways to positively impact individual and team performance is an essential component of true success."

Section IV

Sustaining Soulful-Leadership

$(((\cdot)))$

CHAPTER VII:

Sustaining Soulful-Leadership

As a review here are the foundational traits of a soulful-leader:

- Soulful-leaders respond rather than react to the need for change. That is, they do not have knee jerk reactions but rather thoughtful and intentional responses when the winds of change blow around them.
- Soulful-leaders lead more by asking powerful, discerned questions than handing out demands or telling others what to do.
- Soulful-leaders lead more by example than e-mail.
- Soulful-leaders preserve confidentiality and integrity. They coach by working from the agenda of the person or organization being coached.
- Soulful-leaders encourage and allow storytelling as a way of building community that ultimately co-creates their future or that of the organization.
- Soulful leaders are always learning. Having the attitude, "I am a student and steward of life"! They invest in training, coaching and consulting to be on top of new trends and effective leadership strategies.
- Soulful leaders are accountable.
- Soulful leaders set goals and objectives that are communicated to the entire organization.

- Soulful leaders connect body, mind and soul.
- Soulful leaders flex their spiritual muscles, physical muscles and psychological muscles.

Don't forget to look in the back of the book for a resource list of coaching, consulting and training companies that may fit your needs.

Brian McClaren, a pastor, author and 21st century thought leader captured the essence and impact of the cultural shifts all around us when he penned the following words on his blog at www.deepshift.com.

We Are In Deep Shift.

A time of transition

rethinking

re-imagining

and re-envisioning

A time for asking new questions

and seeking answers

that are both new and old

fresh and seasoned

surprising and familiar

What does it mean, in today's world, to be a follower of God in the way of Jesus?

What does it mean to be a faith community engaged in the holistic, integral mission of God in our world today?

How do we, as individuals and organizations, respond faithfully to the crises facing our world?

What is our duty to God, ourselves, our families, our neighbors, our enemies, and our planet in light of Jesus' radical message of the kingdom of God?

How can we engage in personal formation and theological reformulation for global transformation?

Living in deep shift can be exhilarating and energizing, but it can also be disorienting and frightening.[57]

---

[57] Brian D. McLaren, "We are in Deep Shift," http://deepshift.org/site/?p=16

Capturing Your Stories – Making Your Shifts
Happen!

May I (Eddie) be personal with you for a moment? May I share something of my story with you that describe the shifts I'm facing?

As of this writing, my family has more who have passed from this earth than those of us left on this earth. Many of those of us left are faced with aging bodies, declining health, and moving into retirement years. While this reality brings some grief and loss, it also brings new opportunities and opens new doors as a new season of life unfolds. I look forward to early retirement from denominational and local church service and partnering with colleagues to launch another dimension of a consulting and coaching career. I've tracked cultural shifts professionally for several decades and have applied them to faith communities and have helped many communities make needed shifts to improve their effectiveness and efficiency in light of cultural shifts. During these decades of service, I have found a void for similar services in business and non-profit organizations. The remaining years of my career will be focused on coaching training and coaching services to help leaders and organizations make needed shifts that will ensure effectiveness and fulfillment in accomplishing their mission.

These personal shifts really evolve from those of my family who have passed. They were leaders of passion, committed to making a difference in their occupations or careers. Their departure was felt by the organizations they served, and there were few, if any, who stepped into the gap created by their deaths. I want to help fill the gap and restore countless thousands of workers across the country that are not experiencing fulfillment personally, spiritually, or vocationally in their careers. They want to make an impact but they are only logging hours and waiting for the workday to pass. Restoring others by deepening their soul so they can make deep shifts that will impact others is my future.

I want to watch business owners, and managers wake up with excitement about going to work because they know they will impact others that day! I want to coach leaders who are seeking to break unhealthy or unproductive cycles in life and help them discover what's next and what will light their fire and fuel their hearts with hope and fulfillment! I want to watch businesses discover ways not only to impact the souls of those they employ but to nurture their dreams and hopes in ways the business/organization significantly impacts the soul of the institution and the community in which they serve. What does that look like? I'm not sure ... but I know we can explore together and celebrate those connections we make that empower others!

What then are your stories? What are the deep shifts you are faced with today?

- At home?
- In your family?
- At work?
- At play?
- In your community?

- In your finances?
- In your community of faith?
- In other areas of your life?

Change and transition have a way of overwhelming leaders and organizations and the daily demands of work very often distract leaders and organizations from intentionally discerning and charting the future. While their needs for change might be clear, their honorable daily work must be done. This often leaves little time or energy for creating a future that is filled with hope rather than despair or anxiety. Creating sacred space and a priority to slow down and work on change is essential. This is the power of a coaching relationship. This final chapter is dedicated to principles that are based on the coach approach to introducing and managing change. Over the last decade many major corporations and businesses have been seeking to activate the soul in the workplace. This is evidenced by the vast array of books on the subject and the numerous websites addressing the connection between faith and work. (See appendices). Sustaining soulful-leadership is achieved by preserving and following these principles as work agendas and priorities for resources are decided. This will help sustain and continue to move you forward with intentionality and a future focus.

React or Proactively Respond

When the waves of change begin to roll through a town, organization, business or church, the employees and often the leaders get into a reactive posture. Reaction is often based on emotions or the immediate needs of the moment and is primarily characterized by a knee-jerk reaction without considering the big picture or doing much reflection on the situation. Soulful-leaders take a more proactive response to the waves of change. That is they resist a knee-jerk reaction and take time to reflect, inquire of others their perspectives, and explore the benefits and consequences of the changes that are emerging. Response is based on the core values of the organization, the purposes of the business and the hopes and realities of the future.

Exhibiting patience, discernment, and perseverance makes a difference in tense situations. Reactionary and self-deceptive leadership generates even more anxiety. This unhealthy leadership creates more emotional situations because the group involved or the core values of the organization are ignored or overlooked.

Often the reactionary leader ends up spouting forth demands, requirements and more work out of fear without consideration of the impact on others. The soulful-leader reflects more and asks more questions of the constituents rather than making declarations. He or she is intentional about making decisions and allocating resources that moves the organization forward and seeks the best for all involved whenever possible.

Ask Rather than Tell

A significant distinctive of soulful-leadership is the use of the coach approach in the midst of change. The soulful-leader is motivated by a mental and emotional value shift that impacts their leadership strategies. The soulful-leader believes and trusts that those involved, if healthy and open to coaching, are likely to have some of the answers to the challenges facing the organization in light of likely changes. The soulful-leader believes that inviting others to explore options and discover benefits and consequences themselves creates a collaborative atmosphere. Their peers have a voice and feel empowered. The organization can then benefit from the creative and collective wisdom of those in the organization. Such, more often than not, creates an atmosphere that builds ownership of shifts that might need to happen to effectively deal with the change on the horizon. This atmosphere is a vital ingredient of only making small ripples instead of uncontrollable waves when change presents itself to an individual or an organization.

The realities of this shift in the way leadership is exhibited create a feeling of trust, gratitude, integrity and empowerment. This is because the soulful-leader has been willing to listen to persons involved and invited them in brainstorming possible solutions to the challenges being faced. More often than not a leader's value to an organization increases when soulful-leadership principles are followed, and that leader's integrity is enhanced rather than diminished. Working from a foundation of peer-learning, collaboration and integrity energizes the leader and organization to leap forward in function and effectiveness.

Working From and For Integrity

Integrity among leadership is a rare virtue in today's world. North America has encountered the horrors of Enron scandals, political, educational and ecclesiastical scandals abound. As we write this in early 2023, the news is filled with scandals in Washington, D.C., among politicians on both sides. We are again faced with the national debt crisis, and politicians are again at a stalemate to preserve their own political base, giving little regard to the economic catastrophe in the making if they can't find a middle ground.

Soulful-leaders who work from the coach approach and manifest and value the virtues of a soulful-leader earn and live by integrity. Now, one is not perfect, and mistakes are often made in the heat of rapid change but soulful-leaders often have persons in their circle of friends and colleagues who challenge them with accountability to maintain integrity, to stop and reflect before reacting, and to ask powerful questions rather than just making quick decisions and handing out commands.

Soulful-leaders value human creativity and insights. They believe that human beings confronted by change can become bitter and resentful of the change, or they can become better and resolve to embrace change in ways that improve life. The shifts being created by change generates powerful stories of change and transition by each person impacted by the changes. Soulful-leaders understand that creating forums for these new stories to be shared creates a community of trust, companionship and redemption that restores and celebrates the new and knows how to connect the past to the present and future. Saying goodbye to the old is as important as saying hello to the new, and a soulful-leader works with those involved to experience the power of storytelling.

The Power of Storytelling

Annette Simmons offers organizations many resources and forums for crafting and experiencing the power of storytelling.[58] Soulful-leaders know the power of story. Story is a way of saying goodbye and saying hello. Those powerful coaching questions can help facilitate such peer learning and sharing around significant learnings, discoveries, benefits and consequences encountered by change. Story-telling is the number one means of communicating anything. According to the International Storytelling Center, there are six stories you need to learn how to tell:

- who I am stories,
- why I am here stories,
- my vision story,
- teaching stories,
- values in action stories, and
- "I know what you are thinking" stories. [59]

---

[58] See www.groupprocessingconsulting.com – Whoever tells the Best Story Wins; The Story Factor and Safe Place for Dangerous Truths are some of her newest books. ***I need a list of Simmons' books that you want cited here.***
[59] The Six Stories You Need to Know How to Tell, International Storytelling Center, excerpted from Annette Simmons, The Story Factor: Inspiration, Influence, and Persausion Through Storytelling, http://www.storytellingcenter.com/resources/articles/simmons.htm

Some of the powerful coaching questions might include:

* What are the shifts bringing to you?
* What are the shifts taking from you?
* What causes you to engage at a deeper level?
* What are the benefits of the shifts for you? Others?
* How can we honor our past in the present and future we are creating?
* What is the best version of the new we are creating that you can see now?
* What can you take with you into the new?
* Who are those you want to tell about the new being created?
* What will you tell them?
* What keeps coming to you that you choose to ignore?
* What are the choices you make that keep you stuck?
* How can we make this happen?
* What are the likely benefits?

Sharing our human stories and even seeking where our human stories connect with divine stories creates a powerful community. The community becomes the seedbed for birthing the new, for celebrating the collaborative creation and growing stronger through the challenge of change.

The Power of Community

Community is power. Gaining momentum to let go of the past and move toward the future is enhanced and generated through community. People sharing their hurts and hopes, generated by the waves of change, is essential to create forums for new personal, professional, organizational and spiritual growth.

Change happens in and through community. A community can shape the future through their voice. They can help actually make the changes needed and deepen their ownership as their voice and hopes are addressed. Now certainly, we need to be realistic here — not everyone's preferences are possible, but they are certainly more likely to be heard, if not included, through the powerful voice of the community.

Again, coaching questions can help unleash the power of the community. However, the soulful-leader and coach may offer words of encouragement, hope and affirmation as their peers choose to engage in building the new rather than being enraged over the changes being presented. Soulful-leaders understand that during change people need to be heard, but also need to be encouraged and affirmed. Celebrating their contributions, insights and willingness to move forward means a lot to persons who are losing something in order to gain or contribute to the new. I (Eddie) recently talked with one of my coaching clients who work on staff in a church that was needing to make some classroom changes in order to position them more for numerical growth in their inner city church. We had been coaching around this for several sessions and she called to celebrate a powerful move that was made publicly by one of their older charter members of the church. The elderly lady had a powerful insight as her class discussed the need for them to move so another group could use their room. The charter member stood and voted first in the church business meeting where this decision to move forward and move classes was to be made. She voted in favor of the move. Her influence was powerful. The class members followed her lead. The minister that I was coaching decided this was a vital piece of their church history and she wrote a formal letter affirming the decision made by this lady and her class. The letter was signed by all clergy and committee members and was presented to them in a worship setting and attached to their church history records. What a time of celebration, affirmation, encouragement and empowerment! Community is a powerful teacher and the human and organizational stories need to be shared and celebrated.

Pressing Forward Rather Than Untangling the Past

The power of a soulful-leader is manifested through their leadership skills, their sensitivity, their value of the opinions and contributions of others and their efforts to be more responsive than reactionary. Another valuable characteristic of a soulful-leader is the intention of moving people and organizations forward in keeping with their organizational core values and not being consumed by untangling the past or debating the change. So often, change is forced externally by cultural, economic, demographic, or political new realities. So many individuals and organizations and churches are led by leaders who do not want to hurt their employees or membership so they back away from change and are compliant with staying in their own and their organizations comfort zones. A soulful-leader wants to move forward while listening, being sensitive to, and engaging the voice of peers in decision-making. In reality, though the time often comes when a tough decision has to be made. The collaborative efforts prove insufficient for an array of reasons. The leader has to make what is often a painful and unpopular decision.

A checklist and self-evaluation tool is appropriate here. Where are you in your shifts – your journey toward being a soulful-leader – at work, at home, in recreation, at church, in your community? Rank on the continuums below where you are now by an X and where you want to be in a year with a Y. The premise of the book is that *Making Shifts In Waves of Change* involves the following:

Shifts in you as a leader – Internal shifts allow External shifts around you

Talking _____Listening

Telling _____Asking

Dictating_____Discovery

Assigning_____Inviting

Change_____Change and Transition

Building Barriers_____Building Bridges

Reactive_____Proactive

Alignment_____Attunement

A soulful-leader brings transformation to those they invest in and intentionally touch. Soulful-leaders can make a significant difference and can make shifts without making overwhelming waves if they follow the principles in this book. Again, there are times when there is a call for radical and immediate shifts due to economic or other issues related to unhealthy patterns and people in the organization. Such a person or organization is not usually coachable or responsive to soulful-leadership, and the leaders have to move forward regardless of the opinion of the group. However, if the group stays open to collaboration, exhibits the skills of good and healthy decision-making and moves forward rather than simply fighting or choosing not to let go of the past, then birthing the new is highly likely and can be done without the impact of overwhelming waves. Overwhelming and exponential change that is characteristic of our times calls for the deep conviction of a committed soulful-leader and forward-thinking constituents who desire to build a future for their children and grandchildren. Soulful-leaders are committed to life-long learning — facing new challenges with intellectual curiosity, intentional skill sets and a deep soul. Soulful-leaders also covenant with others to maintain a healthy work-life balance so that we take care of ourselves, allowing us to invest in and empower others. Deepening souls in leaders empower them to make and influence deep shifts and transformations in others. The impact of one soul on another soul — be it individual, family, organization or church, brings transformation of heart, head, healing and hope. What better gift to bring and to be! The impact and influence of soulful-leaders ripples through many and continues to impact for some time. For instance, recall the interviews with the pilot who landed his plane on the Hudson. Family, spouses, children, friends, colleagues, neighbors etc, brought to him words of appreciation and gratitude. The children still had parents, the parents still had children, the grandparents......and the ripples on impact and influence continue.

Hope is birthed by the leaders and visions of those who choose to respond well to meaningful change rather than fight it just to preserve our comfort zones and allow us to rest in the fields of familiarity. Making Shifts In Waves of Change is possible when guided by soulful-leaders and persons with a deep abiding view of the future. What are your next steps as a soulful-leader? Who can help you achieve your dreams and create the new story for your life and organization?

Maybe a fitting conclusion to sustaining soulful-leadership includes when to send out the flare for help. We all have limitations on time, energy or resources when it comes to managing and introducing change. So here's another checklist for you to consider. Send out the cry for help ...

- If you or the organization is stuck
- Inability to be stretched or to stretch others
- Loss of passion or energy for the new
- Feeling of being drained
- More of inward focus than outward focus
- Overwhelming resistance to change
- Doing the same thing over and over and expecting change
- Limited leadership to make needed impact and cast needed influence
- Networking with pioneers who sees and cast transformational ideas
- Need for greater objectivity and outsiders perspectives
- Hire a coach and experience the power of coaching that moves you forward
- Look at it without the clouded emotions or turfism typical of persons in a given organization.

As a final word, Eddie and Randy want to share with our readers in somewhat of a coaching demonstration. Sharing a glimpse of the transformations we have experienced over more than a decade of learning to walk into our fears, challenge our biases and assumptions, and heightening our awareness of personal dysfunctions and unhealthy coping skills while embracing the new dreams planted in our souls.

Epilogue:

Soulful-Leaders Create Transformation

Transformation, Impact, Influence – Personal Journeys

Soulful-leadership is about transformation – not just thinking "outside the box" but living "beyond the box" and therefore positively influencing, impacting and inspiring those around you to live the same.

Remember About 3:35 p.m. on Friday, January 16, 2009, Captain Scully on US Airways flight 1549 made a transforming decision in a given moment in time. The engines of the aircraft had died (apparently due to birds being sucked into the engines upon take-off from Laguardia airport). The plane was already in flight, and the captain and co-captain were now faced with critical decisions. Where do we land? How do we land? When do we land? And how do we protect the 155 persons onboard the plane?

It seems Captain Scully followed the principles of a soulful-leader – he drew from his vast experience, internal discernment, expert skills and trusted his heart, along with his intellect as he reached out for help. He proved that not only could he think "outside the box," but he was willing to live "beyond the box" and follow through on his creative thinking and the counsel of others. Reaching out for help was a key element. The result was what is now being called "Miracle on the Hudson River." The captain and co-captain landed the plane on the Hudson River in a way that was smooth and almost as efficient as it would have landed on the tarmac of the airport. Now certainly, the logical and traditional mode of landing a plane was to land that type of plane on an airport runway. However, in this situation, circumstances suddenly changed and called for another way of landing the plane. There was no time or engine power to take the plane back to the airport. How does the pilot deal with such a challenging situation?

We are told by other pilots and investigators, that the pilot of flight 1549 made the right decision at the right time, and the result was everyone survived the crash! The plane without power glided to a fairly calm landing on the Hudson River. Some might call this living into a "karios moment" – where everything lines up for the perfect plan to come together. Soulful-leaders live to create and experience such moments even though they might often feel it's "beyond the box."

New challenges call for new leadership. For the most part in past decades, leaders led more by gathering information (which changes minute by minute) and being reactive to the information. More so, they led by strategic planning that calls on discernment and trusting the Spirit. Frequently leaders seek to please their community or colleagues rather than decide with the community of the world in mind. Often models of leading are driven by fear and issues of control rather than desires to empower others to experience freedom, fulfillment, hope, and health. Empowering others to follow their dreams, calling, and instinct assures forward movement rather than staying stuck or inward focused.

Captain Scully modeled much of what we mean by soulful-leadership when he trusted the crew, trusted the plane, found and trusted the water and followed his instinct and training which allowed the plane to land on the water and offered much greater chances of a safe landing than trying to return to the known and trusted tarmac. Captain Scully trusted what he knew and he followed his heart in the face of deep challenges. Learning to live "beyond the box" and one's comfort zone is essential in becoming a soulful-leader.

As authors of this book, Randy and Eddie want to share something of their transformation over the last decade.

- What transformations have occurred in the last decade?
- What created these shifts?
- How has the transformation changed your life? Career?
- How have you made the shifts called for?
- What worked?
- What did not work?
- What's next for you now?

A Glimpse into
the Author's Transformation

"Life happens" and "Life is hard" are two clichés that summarize the attitude of many during these challenging days of global and local economic, social, cultural, and organizational shifts. Many become disillusioned, if not resentful, of the shifts that are so often seemingly "beyond our control" or "beyond our reach or pay grade." Our culture is increasingly birthing times and circumstances that call us to newness and transformation. Soulful-leaders create transformation as we create safe places and sometimes, ongoing coaching relationships that are intentional in discerning together next steps and what forward movement will look like now. These are often divine appointments and filled with teachable moments that fuel dreams, inspire change, and open heart, head, and soul for needed shifts to occur. Your authors, Eddie and Randy, have experienced this transformation over the last 25 plus years as we have challenged each other, created safe places for struggles of the soul and now living into dreams. We want to share something of our stories of personal and professional transformation in hopes of inspiring and letting you know we "practice what we teach." Moving from our pinches to our dreams, experiencing a retooling and refreshment of head, heart and soul, and discovering inspiration and hope characterize some of the shifts we want to share with you in this coaching demonstration. We hope this helps you visualize what a coaching relationship might look like – at least a short vignette from our coaching conversations.

Coaching Conversation – Moving from Pain to Purpose

Eddie (coach): *Randy, how would you describe your transformation over the last 25 years?*

Randy (person being coached): My journey has been long, difficult, and painful at times. I have had to learn how to integrate head and heart and push ego out of the way. Many of my coping skills and attitudes needed to be re-framed and re-aligned. At times anger and resentment would motivate me to get things done, but I never felt satisfied or complete. Turning my resentment into gratitude has taken years as I continue to follow what motivates me and fuels my passion. At times this was walking away from a big paycheck and doing other things that allowed me to search internally and begin to see and feel where I was being called to go. I have learned that I must do things that excite me, involve personal relationships, and constant learning. Without a big learning curve, I have found that I get bored and lose my focus and energy.

Eddie (coach): *What has been the power of coaching in your life?*

Randy (person being coached): I am an experiential learner. I need to talk things out and allow myself time to embrace my internal and external shifts. This is the power of coaching for me. Coaching allows me to think out loud in a safe environment with an objective listener. The coach approach is the way of the future in my opinion, but is extremely hard work. If a person really wants to change and make some shifts they must unlearn things they may have been doing for a very long time and replace them with new attitudes, behaviors and skill-sets. This is much easier said than done. It has been my experience that this cannot be done alone, thus the value of a coach.

Eddie (coach): *Randy, how are you living your dream now?*

Randy (person being coached): I never thought about being a coach. Coaching really found me. And I never thought about writing. That is for sure! Living into my dream is about helping others make shifts in their lives to be better and to lead better. I have been blessed to have people in my life help me to see some of the extremely stupid decisions that I have made that at times held me back or would take me in a direction that really was not where I wanted to go. Fear and uncertainty are powerful feelings that at times caused me to be impulsive and reactionary that always led me to painful pinches. I have learned it is certainly OK to fall down and fail. It is part of the process. It really is a process in which everyday I am reminded that I am only as good as my last decision. The power of choice and the collaboration with others allows us to do greater things together than if we simply stand alone.

Eddie (coach): *Thanks for sharing this with us. Now can you summarize what are the characteristics of a soulful-leader you now embody? What are your next steps?*

Randy (person being coached): I am grateful for the shifts that the coaching experience has allowed me that has opened new and exciting doors for me. I plan to continue to walk with courage and know that it is OK to be vulnerable at times. It is in those vulnerable "soft" times that we can make the most shifts in attitudes and behavior. When I become bulletproof, and ego begins to get in the way, I have learned to reach out and admit that this is a red flag for me and is robbing me of the opportunity for authentic conversations and collaboration. Being accountable and stepping outside of the cycle of blame have been two of my biggest shifts. In order to do this I had to embrace surrender and gratitude.

Now we will change roles – for indeed, this has been true for us in these later years, as Randy has received his coach certification, too.

Coaching Conversation
Moving from Telling to Asking

Randy (coach): *Eddie, how would you describe your transformation over the last 25 years?*

Eddie (person being coached): My shifts have been internal and external as well as personal and professional. Early on in our conversations, I felt like I had the answers, and I was to "tell you" and get you to agree with me about issues of faith, life, economics, or whatever the issues might be. Much of my professional training had reinforced this mindset. It was quickly evident to me that this was not working too well in communicating or connecting with you. In fact, the assumption that I had the answers you needed actually sabotaged at times me really being able to hear what you were saying to me. My assumption was that if you would only listen to what I was trying to tell you often prevented me from connecting with you and you connecting with me.

Over time, after butting my head against that wall, out of desperation, I started "asking" questions and soon discovered that at least we could talk without arguing. This epiphany coincided with an invitation to have a coach and to begin to learn something about coaching. WOW — what a discovery and a relief the experience of being coached had for me. I learned what makes a powerful coaching question and what the benefits of coaching had on me making shifts that were transforming to me personally, spiritually and professionally. This shift impacted my home relationships, friendships and the way I functioned in my job as a consultant.

Randy (coach): *What has been the power of coaching in your life?*

Eddie (person being coached): I must confess first of all that I was a real skeptic of the impact of coaching – being that most coaching is done by phone, and I have been such a face-to-face person. But, boy, am I a believer now that coaching by phone with a coach I may never meet face-to-face can be life-changing and career-changing! The experience of having a coach and bringing my personal agenda to each call offered me a focus I've never known. Focus came to my career in ways that empowered, energized and created a retooling that has now birthed 9 books, multiple sources of income, powerful professional relationships beyond my "day job," allowed me to travel across the country, coach business, and church leader clients and fueled me with dreams that allow me to enter each day (well almost every day) with renewed energy and expectation.

Personally, having a coach (and by the way, every coach needs a coach) even now has proven to inspire me, motivate me, and create pathways of being proactive rather than reactive to circumstances. For instance, I had to have major surgery two years ago and faced the threat of death, disability and an extended recovery that, for many patients in similar circumstances, would likely include depression. I chose to hire a coach to walk with me during these months. I am now doing very well – and though my recovery was over a year – I never got depressed. I never lost my zest for life or my vision for my life and career. In fact, I am certain, that those fifteen- to twenty-minute coaching calls (that was all I had energy for) kept me focused on the future enough to keep me out of depression. What a gift those powerful questions were for me during those challenging and often 'dark days'!

Randy (coach): *Eddie, how are you living your dream now?*

Eddie (person being coached): This book is evidence of living my dream. I have wanted to work with you in ways that would share with a larger audience the discoveries we have helped each other make over the last decades. The overwhelming success of our first writing collaboration, the follow-up seminars and workshops, then the occasional articles and the coaching sessions we do together have given me "new wind in my sails" and have proven to me that our journey – as difficult as it has been some days – is not without meaning and purpose.

I'm also living my dream of influencing more consistently those in the day-to-day grind and challenges of family life and work life. So many can benefit from the forward focus of coaching rather than wrestling with the untangling of the past, that often is the route of counseling these stressed or stuck workers pursue. I am convinced that these challenging and changing times in which we now live are prime opportunities and fertile fields for coaching to impact lives, restore dreams, and retool businesses and organizations to a more fulfilling experience.

Randy (coach): *Thanks for sharing this with us. Now can you summarize what are the characteristics of a soulful-leader you now embody? What are your next steps?*

Eddie (person being coached): My next steps are to continue my coaching and coach training and explore new avenues of its power and impact. I also plan to continue my consulting with organizations – profit and non-profit as I seek to make a difference in the world and help organizations, families, and leaders make shifts without making too many unnecessary waves. My personal transformation continues as I learn to live by the lessons I have learned through the tough times and celebrations of life and career. The power of coaching continues to invite me to see my divine destiny and to walk into it without fear.

* * *

Change has indeed come to America and the world in this decade. Families, companies, churches and communities are learning to live by and through new challenges and opportunities. What kind of world would we live in if we have transformed leaders and families transforming the institutions and organizations they are a part of? The choice is ours as soulful leaders. We are called to make the right decisions or make our decisions right. What is your decision?

Appendices

Coaching Model for Making Shifts In Waves of Change

(The Harmony Model)

Hearing Others
- Who needs to be in the conversation?
- What are their assumptions about the challenge?
- What's the best setting that assures them they are being heard?
- How can we best listen to them?

Assessing the Situation to find focus
- What are the pinches here?
- What is really going on?
- What will it take to move forward for each person/group?

Responding to Questions/Concerns
- What do you need to know now?
- What are your primary concerns/questions?
- What is needed now?
- Who can help you with your concerns/questions?

Movement forward decisions by the group
- What will move us forward in this dialogue now?
- What are the criteria for a good decision?
- How can we help each other now?

- What is needed by each person in the group now?
- How can we help each other now?
- Who else can you share your insights with now?

Options to explore to build ownership
- What are the possibilities here?
- What options are before us?
- What are the consequences of exploring each option?
- What are the benefits of exploring each option?
- Who can help us with these explorations?
- What are the criteria needed to make the best decisions now?
- What would it look like to follow through on each option?

Negotiating Next Steps from previous conversations
- How can we move on now?
- How would you summarize where we are now?
- What are the next steps needed?
- Who can help with taking the next steps?
- What is the timeline best for us?
- What are the consequences of not moving forward now?

Yes voices frame the next steps
- What have we decided?
- How would you summarize what we have heard from others?
- What is needed now?
- How does what we have heard inform our future?
- How can we celebrate our consensus?

Tool Kit for Soulful-Leaders and Soulful-Organizations

- Pain to Purpose Model
- Wandering to Walking Model

Coaching Bibliography

Compiled by Eddie Hammett, MCC

Blackstock, Terri. The Listener: What if You Could Hear What God Hears. Nashville: Westbow Press, 2000.

Cameron, Julia. The Listening Path, The Creative Art of Attention. New York: St Martins Publishing Co,2021

Chamine, Shirazad. Positive Intelligence: Why Only 20% of Teams and Individuals Achieve Their True Potential. Austin, TX: Greenleaf Press, 2016.

Clark, Dorie. Reinventing You: Define Your Brand, Imagine Your Future. Boston: Harvard Business Review, 2013.

Clark, Dorie. Entrepreneurial You: Monetize Your Expertise. Boston: Harvard Business Review Press, 2017.

Crane, Thomas. The Heart of Coaching: Using Transformational Coaching to Create High-Performance Culture. San Diego: FTA Press, 2002

Creswell. Jane. Benefits of Christian Coaching for Ministry Leaders.St Louis: Lake Hickory Resources, 2006.

Drake, David. Narrative Coaching: Bringing Our New Stories into Life. California, CNC Press, 2018.

Flaherty, James. Coaching: Evoking Excellence in Others. Boston: Butterworth, Heinemann, 2003.

Glaser, Judith. Conversational Intelligence: How Great Leaders Build Trust and Get Extraordinary Results. New York: Bibliomotion, 2014.

Goleman, Daniel. FOCUS: The Hidden Driver of Excellence. Boston. Harper, 2015.

Goldsmith, Marshall. What Got You Here Won't Get You There, New York: Hyperion Books, 2007.

Gupta, Sanjay. Keep Sharp: Build a Better Brain at Any Age. New York; Simon & Schuster, 2021

Hargrove, Robert. Masterful Coaching: Inspire an "Impossible Future"While Producing Extraordinary Leaders and Extraordinary Results. San Francisco: Jossey Bass-Pfiffer, 2003

Johnson, Whitney. Build An A-Team: Play to Their Strengths and Lead Them Up the Learning Curve. New York: Harvard Business Review. 2018.

Johnson, Whitney. Disrupt Yourself: Putting the Disruptive Innovation to Work. New York: Bibliomotion Press, 2015.

Johnson, Whitney. Dare, Dream, Do: Remarkable Things Happen When You Dare to Dream. New York: Bibliomotion Press, 2012.

Joly, Herbert. The Heart of Business: Leadership for the Next-Era of Capitalism. New York: Harvard Business Review, 2021.

McDonald, Gordon. A Resilient Life: You Can Move Ahead No Matter What. Nashville: Thomas Nelson Publisher, 2004.

Miller, Linda and Madeleine Holman. Coaching in Organizations: Best Coaching Practices San Francisco, Ken Blanchard Co., 2008

Pagan, Eben. Opportunity: How to Win in Business & Create a Life You Love. California: Hay House Publisher, 2019.

Reynolds, Marcia. The Discomfort Zone: How Leaders Turn Difficult Conversations into Breakthroughs. San Francisco: Berrett-Koehler Publisher, 2014.

Reynolds, Marcia. Coach the Person, Not the Problem: A Guide to Using Reflective Inquiry, San Francisco: Berrett-Koeholer, 2020.

Stanier, Michael Bungay. The Coaching Habit: Say, Less, Ask More and Change the Way You Lead Forever. Canada: Page Two, 2016.

Stanier, Michael Bungay. The Advice Trap: Be Humble, Stay Curious and Change the Way You Lead Forever. Canada: Box of Crayons Press, 2020.

Stoltzfus, Tony. Leadership Coaching: The Disciplines, Skills, and Heart of a Coach. Va Beach, 2005.

Prepared 2/15/2023

Possible Coaching Questions for Making Shifts in Waves of Change

Coaching Questions to Consider:

- What emotions scare you?

- What emotions do you feel that you cannot label?

- What have you been looking for in life but have not found?

- What are your pursuits now?

- What would be the impact of living life as to not have 'bad experiences?

- How would you grow a soul that radiates health?

- What is the best expression of your faith in your work?

- What is your typical reaction/behavior when you are sad or angry? Does this at times feel out of control?

- Do you hide things from others and often lie to yourself and others?   How would you describe this behavior healthy or unhealthy?

- How can you become more honest, as you begin to step out of denial, and strengthen your true self?

- What habit changes would improve your life?   Which ones? Which ones are you willing to change now?

- What old tapes play over and over in your mind that sabotage your future and keep you stuck?

- What new tapes can start playing over your old tapes that propel you forward to health and wholeness?

- Are you a person who always needs to be right? Does it upset you to compromise?

- What could help you begin to see things through different lenses if needed?

- Are you willing to change to move towards happiness?

Questions may be:

- What is really going on?

- What are the pinches here?

- What are the resources needed to move forward?

Coaching Models for Soulful-Leaders

From Pain to Purpose

From Stuck to Unstuck

From Wandering to Walking

From Success to Significance

From Maintenance to Mission to Capacity Building

- **B** ullet proof

- **A** voidance

- **R** esistance

- **R** oad blocks

- **I** mpulse

- **E** go

- **R** esentment

- **S** abotage

Coaching Models for Soulful-Leaders

From Pain to Purpose

From Stuck to Unstuck

From Wandering to Walking

From Success to Significance

From Maintenance to Mission to Capacity Building

- **B** elief Systems

- **R** elationships

- **I** ntention

- **D** iscover

- **G** ifts

- **E** ngagement

- **S** ummarize

Basic Coaching Model

- Focus

- Action

- Summary

- Tracking

Basic Coaching Skills

- Listen

- Encourage

- Ask powerful questions

- Respond

- Negotiate action

Coaching to FACE Change

- F ear

- Accept

- Community

- Evaluate/Explore

Coaching to MAKE Change

- Movement

- Adjust

- Kinesis

- Evolve

Coaching to EMBRACE Change

- **E**xperiment

- **M**anage/Maintain

- **B**ridges/Barriers

- **R**ebuild

- **A**lign

- **C**hallenge

- **E**xplode

Revolutionary Transformation =
Change + Transition.

LIST OF OTHER BOOKS BY EDWARD HAMMETT

- Reaching People Under 30 While Keeping People Over 60

- Coaching As Spiritual Practice: Deepening Faith While Deeping Impact

- The Gathered and Scattered Church: Equipping Believers for the 21st Century

- Reframing Spiritual Formation: Discipleship in an Unchurched Culture

- Making the Church Work: Converting the Church for the 21st Century

- Recovering Hope for Your Church: Moving beyond Maintenance and Missional to Incarnational Engagement

- Spiritual Leadership in a Secular Age: Building Bridges Instead of Barriers

All books are listed on Amazon.com under the name Edward H. Hammett